Selected Writings of
JOHN RUSKIN

SELECTED WRITINGS
OF
JOHN
RUSKIN

*Edited
and Introduced by*
PETER QUENNELL

LONDON

THE FALCON PRESS

First published in 1952
by the Falcon Press (London) Limited
6 & 7 Crown Passage, Pall Mall,
London, S.W.1
Printed in Great Britain
by The Alcuin Press
Welwyn Garden City

CONTENTS

From *Praeterita* 1885-1889

INTRODUCTION BY PETER QUENNELL

JOHN RUSKIN'S FIRST ATTEMPT TO COMPOSE A WORK OF English literature was begun during the autumn months of 1826 and finished 'about January 1827'. The author, who was still in his seventh year, carefully copied his whole composition into a little red-bound blue-ruled note-book, using a special script that imitated book-print, with his own line-drawings interspersed to suggest contemporary copper-plates. After a life of prodigious activity, he wrote his last paragraph while he was recovering from a grave illness in the summer of 1889. Both productions are highly characteristic—*Harry and Lucy Concluded*, his earliest work, of Ruskin's strange mixture of imaginative and scientific tendencies, 'the interwoven temper of my mind, at the beginning of days just as much as at their end': *Joanna's Care*, with which he brought to a close his rambling reminiscences, of that exquisite feeling for natural beauty which throughout his life had haunted him. He was writing of the fireflies near Siena:

> *How* they shone! moving like fine-broken starlight through the purple leaves. How they shone! through the sunset that faded into thunderous night ... the white edges of the mountainous clouds still lighted from the west. ... The fire-flies everywhere in sky and cloud rising and falling, mixed with the lightning and more intense than the stars.

There the pen seems literally to have dropped from his hand; for, although Ruskin lived on until January 1900, an antique and mysterious figure, neatly arrayed in old-fashioned clothes, with double-breasted waistcoat, heavy gold watch-chain and

vii

the broad azure cravat which matched his bright blue eyes, brooding among his favourite Turners or wandering on his valet's arm around his terraced gardens, any effort—even the effort of framing a brief note—had at length become impossible. But to his credit was a monumental pile of essays, studies, lectures; and, during one of the most devoted and industrious careers of which history keeps a record, his prose had constantly changed and developed according to the interior changes of the writer's personality. For style is an organic growth—a fact that cannot be too frequently remembered, either by those who aspire to stylistic excellence or by authors so impressed with the value of what they have to say that the problem of how to say it appears scarcely worth their interest. Style reflects the evolutionary processes of an individual mind and heart, as soon as it ceases to do so degenerating into mannerism; and Ruskin's prose from youth to old age followed the pattern of his inward life, graceful and elaborate when he was young and sanguine, austere and trenchant as the sense of public responsibility slowly gained upon him, reflective and nostalgic once he had given up his life's struggle and was resigned to living in the past, while a generation of which he despaired swept forward to its dubious fate.

The present selection, indeed, reflects three different Ruskins: the high-minded 'Graduate of Oxford' who delighted his parents and impressed the world by producing the first volume of *Modern Painters* in April 1843; the angry prophet who grieved his father and enraged Victorian book-critics by publishing *Unto This Last* towards the end of 1860; and the old man, his hopes spent and his passions almost worn out, whose discursive autobiography, which he called *Praeterita*, began to take shape in 1885. Yet, although strikingly dissimilar, these three aspects of the stylist had a well-established common background. None of his experiences in adult life could weaken the effect of the writer's early training—of lessons at his mother's

knee where every day of his childish existence he read and repeated and learned by heart long passages of the English Bible;
and of candle-lit evenings in the family parlour, listening to his
father read aloud from one of Sir Walter Scott's historical
romances. Scott was a novelist he continued to revere.

> I am ... [he declared in *Praeterita*] ... a violent Tory of the
> old school; (Walter Scott's school ... and Homer's,) I name
> these two out of the numberless great Tory writers, because they
> were my own two masters. I had Walter Scott's novels, and the
> *Iliad* (Pope's translation,) for my only reading when I was a
> child, on week-days: on Sundays their effect was tempered by
> Robinson Crusoe and the Pilgrim's Progress. ...

With such masters, he afterwards considered, he had avoided
many pitfalls:

> ... once knowing the 32nd of Deuteronomy, the 119th Psalm,
> the 15th of 1st Corinthians, the Sermon on the Mount, and
> most of the Apocalypse, every syllable by heart, and having
> always a way of thinking with myself what words meant, it was
> not possible for me, even in the foolishest times of youth, to
> write entirely superficial or formal English

by which he meant the stately Latinate prose of Edward Gibbon and Samuel Johnson, authors whom he could not learn to
appreciate, since their use of language struck him as cold and
harsh and lifeless. Later he developed a fervent admiration for
the prose of Richard Hooker, deciding that 'for the purposes of
argument ... Hooker's English was the perfectest existing
model'; but at the same time he admired the colloquial prose
of Byron, noting its vigorous masculine fluency and the
compression of meaning that Byron achieved in a single
happy epithet. Byron's letters, he announced, were often '*perfect*' because the quantity of sense they enclosed was

> ... not artificially or intricately concentrated, but with the
> serene swiftness of a smith's hammerstrokes on hot iron; and

with choice of terms which, each in its place, will convey far more than they mean in the dictionary.

These were the models to whom he had vowed fidelity. As long as he was capable of holding a pen, their admonitions still pursued him.

In his books, what was the combined result? A style that at its most decorative was never loosely florid: at its most sententious and dogmatic, never insensitive or clumsy. Its operations, as I have already suggested, fall into three main literary periods, of which the first opened with a series of architectural essays, signed 'Kataphusin' and published in the *Architectural Magazine* while he was yet at Oxford, and with the appearance of *Modern Painters*, Vol. 1, during the spring of 1843. Ruskin was living at his parents' house. Having surmounted a major emotional crisis and a serious physical breakdown, he was the spoiled darling of his mother and father who supervised his health and happiness with tremulous solicitude. To them he would read his work aloud; and 'they used both to cry a little, at least my father did, over the pretty passages, when I read them after breakfast'. Originally a vindication of Turner's genius, *Modern Painters* gradually extended its scope as visits to foreign picture-galleries enlarged the writer's point of view, and was not definitely rounded off till the publication of the last volume during the course of 1860. Hard on the heels of its second volume came *Seven Lamps of Architecture*, which prompted him to plunge deeper into architectural studies, focusing his attention upon a single city. *The Stones of Venice* reached his admirers in the early spring of 1851.

During the intervals much had occurred to puzzle and distract him. He had married in a gust of passion, and his marriage had proved to be an ignominious failure. His wife left him and obtained an annulment; and it was a saddened and disillusioned man who in 1854, after a brief spell of relative independence, returned to his parents' shadow and the life of filial servitude.

Thus, although *Modern Painters* remained unfinished until 1860, Ruskin's first period of writing may be said to have lasted from 1843 to 1854—a period during which he wrote for the most part in the grand manner, employed all his literary artifice and was lavish of the 'pretty passages' that caused James Ruskin to shed admiring tears. How far these passages were merely 'pretty' a reader must decide on his own account as he examines some famous specimens printed in the following pages. Against 'fine writing' and the cult of the 'purple passage' (vulgarized before Ruskin's death by undiscriminating admirers of the prose of Walter Pater) a prejudice, not altogether reasonable, has sprung up in the last half-century. Fine writing is judged effeminate: elaborate stylistic flights are brushed aside as otiose. To this line of attack one can only reply that the writer who clings to a style of uncoloured flat colloquialism must necessarily limit himself to a very narrow range of interests. He may describe the spectacle that meets his eyes; but, lacking the resources of rhythm and verbal variety, he cannot hope to convey those subtle over-tones of emotion which give the experience its proper value. Ruskin's purpose in writing was both instructive and evocative. His prose flights are never irrelevant, but rise spontaneously with the subject or group of subjects with which he was preoccupied. The admirable habit, learned in childhood, of always 'thinking with myself what words meant', and never allowing his images to blur into hazy picturesqueness, is as much in evidence in his early and romantic, as in his later and more dogmatic, prose; and his celebrated descriptions of the Square of St. Mark's—contrasted so ingeniously with a sober English cathedral-close —and of the beggars and vagrant children sprawled around the church porch, are as precisely detailed and sharply evocative as his command of words can make them. Every phrase has a definite task to perform. Not an adjective is misplaced.

For here was a critic passionately devoted to beauty—not

only to the beauty of words, the formal magnificence of buildings, statues, pictures, but to the whole visible universe as it unfolded round him: the grace of a swarthy beggar-girl, the instinctive elegance with which a young woman arranged her braids and bonnet, a spotted snail-shell on the sands of the Lido, flowers in an Italian orchard or the cloud-scapes above Coniston Water. His genius had a strongly sensuous cast; and so immediate and so acute were the pleasures he experienced that, mindful of his parents' puritan training, he often doubted if such pagan delights were altogether justified. As he grew older, his native distrust of happiness grew more and more perceptible, and, to complicate his private *malaise*, a deep sense of social wrong little by little began to colour all writings. Horrified by the evidences of social injustice—by the degradation of the London poor and the squalor of the new industrial towns— he decided, nobly but perhaps unwisely, that he must seek to combat them. He could no longer rest and enjoy the pleasures of the mind till he had offered his own contribution towards rebuilding England.

Ruskin's motives were usually mixed; and there is no doubt that his protests against society had a partly personal basis. His personal life having gone miserably awry—he yearned for the warmth of human love; and love and the glow of satisfied passion were perpetually denied him—he tended to divert his dissatisfaction into altruistic channels. Yet his disinterestedness cannot be denied. When he published the three opening chapters of *Unto This Last* in the *Cornhill Magazine*, a new monthly periodical edited by Thackeray, he occupied an exceedingly enviable position among contemporary writers. He was the English art critic *par excellence*, looked up to by the young, respected by his elders; and from that position he proceeded to abdicate with a single daring essay. *Unto This Last* was a widely unpopular book; few copies were bought by the public, and its unpopularity had a damaging effect upon the sale of previous volumes. *Bosh!* exclaimed Rossetti, the intransigent artist who had no use for social theories: the ravings of a 'mad governess', declared an angry leader-writer. Ruskin, in fact, struck at the very foundations of British prosperity and British self-complacency, daring to question the least humane yet most deeply rooted of Victorian economic doctrines. Poverty, had announced the Manchester School, was the price we must expect to pay for the rate of modern progress, since it was the result of a 'natural law', and any attempt to curtail that law—by cutting off the industrialist from his supply of cheap labour, or attempting to raise the labourer's wages to an artificial level—might inflict irreparable harm on the entire commercial structure, thus plunging the labouring masses into utter destitution. Calmly but firmly Ruskin begged to doubt both the wisdom and the morality of Manchester economists. The labourer, he protested, was a creature of spirit, who would neither work like a machine nor could be relegated to the status of an economic cipher; and for his pains he was immediately denounced as an interfering malcontent or revolutionary hot-head. During the whole of the prophet's middle life, his prestige among the educated reading public did not quite recover.

If Ruskin's main aesthetic period may be dated approximately from 1843 to 1854, his prophetic phase, which opened in 1860, covered more than two decades. During his youth a stern moralist had sometimes jogged the aesthete's elbow; but, after the publication of *Unto This Last*, it was the prophet and soothsayer who invariably took the first place. His activities during that stage of his career were varied and incessant. He wrote on a score of subjects; he lectured, taught and proselytized, always earnestly and vehemently, very often angrily; but, as his indignation grew more intense and his range of subjects wider, his faculty of concentration revealed a steady falling-off. He found it difficult to stick to the theme he had chosen, so dense was the throng of ideas struggling for utterance; and a tone of feverish unhealthy excitement began to creep into his prose style. Yet even now his mastery of language appeared in many passages. *Fors Clavigera*, a long succession of open letters addressed to the workmen of Great Britain, contains much that is repetitive and some sections, written towards the end, that are almost unintelligible. Yet again and again lucidity broke forth in simple trenchant paragraphs, as, for example, in his dramatic picture of the sweated English nail-makers—'ominous *Clavigerae*', toiling, the whole family of them, throughout the hours of daylight for less than £60 a year—which is printed in this selection on page 99.

Every reader knows how the period concluded: how, overwhelmed by the weight of private frustration and public disappointments, his reason finally succumbed in the early months of 1878. He emerged from the shadows of insanity, only once again to plumb their depths. Brain-storm succeeded brainstorm; but between these recurrent crises he was usually calm and rational; and after his fourth breakdown, during such a spell of calm, he embarked upon *Praeterita*. It was the masterpiece of Ruskin's old age, just as *Modern Painters* and *The Stones of Venice* had been the triumphant expressions of his energetic and aspiring youth. Then he had looked forward, full of the proud belief that his creative life was dedicated, conscious that he had a noteworthy task to perform which, thanks to the talents he had inherited, he was not incapable of mastering. But in *Praeterita* he was content to look back—towards scenes far more real to him than the darkened landscape of the present day, reviewing the course of his early life with a rare and delightful combination of tenderness and frankness. He had adored his parents: he had revolted against them: now, himself an elderly man, he could afford to study that odd, devoted, misguided couple quietly and dispassionately. Maybe their exclusive devotion had crippled his development. Well, the harm had been done and was past all cure, just as he was past all indignation. From the ashes of the burnt-out prophet rose once more the artist. *Praeterita* is the most enjoyable of Ruskin's books; for although its tone is gentler and simpler than that of the productions of his middle period, and its cadences less elaborately contrived than those of *Modern Painters* and *The Stones of Venice*, it is evidently the work of the same hand, a hand that in 1885 had not yet lost its precision and its delicacy. But during the next four years his energies dwindled, and the completion of the last chapter required a painful effort. The earlier chapters are clearly the best, the later sections of the narrative being somewhat loosely strung together, with numerous omissions and some suppressions—there is no reference, for example, to the fact that he had married—and little attempt to weld his material into a consecutive life-story. But, as it stands, the book has an incomparable charm. Were *Praeterita* his sole achievement, Ruskin's reputation would still rest upon a firm and lofty pedestal.

In the present anthology I have endeavoured to make a fairly representative, though necessarily incomplete, selection of Ruskin's multitudinous prose-writings, with emphasis not so much on the doctrines he professed or the message that he sought to propagate (though some trace of his theories and prejudices appears through almost every paragraph) as on Ruskin the master of English prose, the imaginative interpreter of art and nature in whom a great French novelist, Marcel Proust, claimed to have recognized his own intercessory guardian-spirit—on the visionary enraptured by the beauty of the world, whose evocation of that fluid, inconstant, always renewed and always changing beauty gives him his especial place among European artist-seers.

PETER QUENNELL

To
MARGARET
with love

OF THE OPEN SKY

IT IS A STRANGE THING HOW LITTLE IN GENERAL PEOPLE know about the sky. It is the part of creation in which Nature has done more for the sake of pleasing man, more for the sole and evident purpose of talking to him and teaching him, than in any other of her works, and it is just the part in which we least attend to her. There are not many of her other works in which some more material or essential purpose than the mere pleasing of man is not answered by every part of their organization; but every essential of the sky might, so far as we know, be answered if once in three days, or thereabouts, a great, ugly, black rain-cloud were brought up over the blue, and everything well watered, and so all left blue again till next time, with perhaps a film of morning and evening mist for dew. And instead of this, there is not a moment of any day of our lives, when Nature is not producing scene after scene, picture after picture, glory after glory, and working still upon such exquisite and constant principles of the most perfect beauty, that it is quite certain that it is all done for us, and intended for our perpetual pleasure. And every man, wherever placed, however far from other sources of interest or of beauty, has this doing for him constantly. The noblest scenes of the earth can be seen and known but by few. It is not intended that man should live always in the midst of them; he injures them by his presence, he ceases to feel them if he be always with them; but the sky is for all; bright as it is, it is not

> Too bright or good
> For human nature's daily food;

it is fitted in all its functions for the perpetual comfort and exalting of the heart, for soothing it and purifying it from its dross and dust. Sometimes gentle, sometimes capricious, sometimes awful, never the same for two moments together; almost human in its passions, almost spiritual in its tenderness, almost divine in its infinity, its appeal to what is immortal in us is as distinct as its ministry of chastisement or of blessing to what is mortal is essential. And yet we never attend to it. We never make it a subject of thought, but as it has to do with our animal sensations: we look upon all by which it speaks to us more clearly than to brutes, upon all which bears witness to the intention of the Supreme that we are to receive more from the covering vault than the light and the dew which we share with the weed and the worm, only as a succession of meaningless and monotonous accident, too common and too vain to be worthy of a moment of watchfulness, or a glance of admiration. If in our moments of utter idleness, and insipidity, we turn to the sky as a last resource, which of its phenomena do we speak of? One says it has been wet; and another, it has been windy; and another, it has been warm. Who, among the whole chattering crowd can tell me of the forms and the precipices of the chain of tall white mountains that girded the horizon at noon yesterday? Who saw the narrow sunbeam that came out of the south and smote upon their summits until they melted and mouldered away in a dust of blue rain? Who saw the dance of the dead clouds when the sunlight left them last night, and the west wind blew them before it like withered leaves? All has passed, unregretted as unseen; or if the apathy be ever shaken off, even for an instant, it is only by what is gross, or what is extraordinary; and yet it is not in the broad and fierce manifestations of the elemental energies, not in the clash of the hail, nor the drift of the whirlwind, that the highest characters of the sublime are developed. God is not in the earthquake, nor in the fire, but in the still, small voice. They are but the blunt and the low faculties of our nature, which can only be addressed through lampblack and lightning. It is in quiet and subdued passages of unobtrusive majesty, the deep, and the calm, and the perpetual; that which must be sought ere it is seen, and loved ere it is understood; things which the angels work out for us daily, and yet vary eternally: which are never wanting, and never repeated; which are to be found always, yet each found but once; it is through these that the lesson of devotion is chiefly taught, and the blessing of beauty given. These are what the artist of highest aim must study; it is these, by the combination of which his ideal is to be created; these, of which so little notice is ordinarily taken by common observers that I fully believe, little as people in general are concerned with art, more of their ideas of sky are derived from pictures than from reality; and that if we could examine the conception formed in the minds of most educated persons when we talk of clouds it would frequently be found composed of fragments of blue and white reminiscences of the old masters.

...OF THE REGION OF THE CIRRUS

OUR NEXT SUBJECT OF INVESTIGATION MUST BE THE specific character of clouds, a species of truth which is especially neglected by artists; first, because as it is within the limits of possibility that a cloud may assume almost any form, it is difficult to point out, and not always easy to feel, wherein error consists; and secondly, because it is totally impossible to study the forms of clouds from Nature with care and accuracy, as a change in the subject takes place between every touch of the following pencil, and parts of an outline sketched at different instants cannot harmonize, Nature never having intended them to come together. Still if artists were more in the habit of sketching clouds rapidly, and as accurately as possible in the outline, from Nature, instead of daubing down what they call 'effects' with the brush, they would soon find there is more beauty about their forms than can be arrived at by any random felicity of invention, however brilliant, and more essential character than can be violated without incurring the charge of falsehood—falsehood as direct and definite, though not as traceable, as error in the less varied features of organic form.

The first and most important character of clouds is dependent on the different altitudes at which they are formed. The atmosphere may be conveniently considered as divided into three spaces, each inhabited by clouds of specific character altogether different, though, in reality, there is no distinct limit fixed between them by Nature, clouds being formed at *every* altitude, and partaking according to their altitude, more or less of the characters of the upper or lower regions. The scenery of the sky is thus formed of an infinitely graduated series of systematic

4

forms of cloud, each of which has its own region in which alone it is formed, and each of which has specific characters which can only be properly determined by comparing them as they are found clearly distinguished by intervals of considerable space. I shall therefore consider the sky as divided into three regions: the upper region, or region of the cirrus; the central region, or region of the stratus; the lower region, or the region of the rain-cloud.

The clouds which I wish to consider as included in the upper region, never touch even the highest mountains of Europe, and may therefore be looked upon as never formed below an elevation of at least 15,000 feet; they are the motionless multitudinous lines of delicate vapour with which the blue of the open sky is commonly streaked or speckled after several days of fine weather. I must be pardoned for giving a detailed description of their specific characters, as they are of constant occurrence in the works of modern artists, and I shall have occasion to speak frequently of them in future parts of the work. Their chief characters are:

First, Symmetry. They are nearly always arranged in some definite and evident order, commonly in long ranks reaching sometimes from the zenith to the horizon, each rank composed of an infinite number of transverse bars of about the same length, each bar thickest in the middle, and terminating in a traceless vaporous point at each side; the ranks are in the direction of the wind, and the bars of course at right angles to it; these latter are commonly slightly bent in the middle. Frequently two systems of this kind, indicative of two currents of wind, at different altitudes, intersect each other, forming a network. Another frequent arrangement is in groups of excessively fine, silky, parallel fibres, commonly radiating, or having a tendency to radiate, from one of their extremities, and terminating in a plumy sweep at the other; these are vulgarly known as 'mares' tails'. The plumy and expanded extremity of these is often bent upwards, sometimes back and up again, giving an appearance of great flexibility and unity at the same time; as if the clouds were tough, and would hold together however bent. The narrow extremity is invariably turned to the wind, and the fibres are parallel with its direction. The upper clouds always fall into some modification of one or other of these arrangements. They thus differ from all other clouds, in having a plan and system; whereas other clouds, though there are certain laws which they cannot break, have yet perfect freedom from anything like a relative and general system of government. The upper clouds are to the lower, what soldiers on parade are to a mixed multitude; no men walk on their heads or their hands, and so there are certain laws which no clouds violate; but there is nothing, except in the upper clouds, resembling symmetrical discipline.

Secondly, Sharpness of Edge. The edges of the bars of the upper clouds which are turned to the wind, are often the sharpest which the sky shows; no outline whatever of any other kind of cloud, however marked and energetic, ever approaches the delicate decision of these edges. The outline of a black thundercloud is striking, from the great energy of the colour or shade of the general mass; but as a line, it is soft and indistinct, compared with the edge of the cirrus in a clear sky with a brisk breeze. On the other hand, the edge of the bar turned away from the wind is always soft, often imperceptible, melting, into the blue interstice between it and its next neighbour. Commonly, the sharper one edge is, the softer is the other; and the clouds looked flat, and as if they slipped over each other like the scales of a fish. When both edges are soft, as is always the case when the sky is clear and windless, the clouds look solid, round, and fleecy.

Thirdly, Multitude. The delicacy of these vapours is sometimes carried into such an infinity of division, that no other sensation of number that the earth or heaven can give is so impressive. Number is always most felt when it is symmetrical (*vide* Burke on *Sublime*, part ii, sect. 8), and, therefore, no sea-waves nor fresh leaves make their number so evident or so impressive as these vapours. Nor is nature content with an infinity of bars or lines alone; each bar is in its turn severed into a number of small undulatory masses, more or less connected according to the violence of the wind. When this division is merely affected by undulation, the cloud exactly resembles sea-sand ribbed by the tide; but when the division amounts to real separation we have the mottled or mackerel skies. Commonly, the greater the division of its bars, the broader and more shapeless is the rank or field, so that in the mottled sky it is lost altogether, and we have large irregular fields of equal size, masses like flocks of sheep; such clouds are 3,000 or 4,000 feet below the legitimate cirrus. I have seen them cast a shadow on Mont Blanc at sunset, so that they must descend nearly to within 15,000 feet of the earth.

Fourthly, Purity of Colour. The nearest of these clouds, those over the observer's head, being at least three miles above him, and the greater number of those which enter the ordinary sphere of vision, farther from him still, their dark sides are much greyer and cooler than those of other clouds, owing to their distance. They are composed of the purest aqueous vapour, free from all foulness of earthly gases, and of this in the lightest and most ethereal state in which it can be, to be visible. Farther, they receive the light of the sun in a state of far greater intensity than lower objects, the beams being transmitted to them through atmospheric air far less dense, and wholly unaffected by mist, smoke, or any other impurity. Hence, their colours are more pure and vivid, and their white less sullied than those of any other clouds.

Lastly, Variety. Variety is never so conspicuous, as when it is united with symmetry. The perpetual change of form in other clouds is monotonous in its very dissimilarity, nor is

7

difference striking where no connection is implied; but if through a range of barred clouds crossing half the heaven, all governed by the same forces and falling into one general form, there be yet a marked and evident dissimilarity between each member of the great mass—one more finely drawn, the next more delicately moulded, the next more gracefully bent, each broken into differently modelled and variously numbered groups—the variety is doubly striking, because contrasted with the perfect symmetry of which it forms a part. Hence, the importance of the truth, that Nature never lets one of the members of even her most disciplined groups of cloud be like another; but though each is adapted for the same function, and in its great features resembles all the others, not one, out of the millions with which the sky is chequered, is without a separate beauty and character, appearing to have had distinct thought occupied in its conception, and distinct forces in its production; and in addition to this perpetual invention, visible in each member of each system, we find systems of separate cloud intersecting each other, the sweeping lines mingled and interwoven with the rigid bars, these in their turn melting into banks of sand-like ripple and flakes of drifted and irregular foam; under all, perhaps the massy outline of some lower cloud moves heavily across the motionless buoyancy of the upper lines, and indicates at once their elevation and their repose.

OF THE REGION OF THE RAIN-CLOUD

THE CLOUDS WHICH I WISH TO CONSIDER AS CHARACTER-istic of the lower, or rainy region, differ not so much in their real nature from those of the central and uppermost regions, as in appearance, owing to their greater nearness. For the central clouds, and perhaps even the high cirri, deposit moisture, if not distinctly rain, as is sufficiently proved by the existence of snow on the highest peaks of the Himalayas; and when, on any such mountains, we are brought into close contact with the central clouds, we find them little differing from the ordinary rain-cloud of the plains, except by being slightly less dense and dark. But the apparent differences, dependent on proximity, are most marked and important.

In the first place, the clouds of the central region have, as has been before observed, pure and aerial greys for their dark sides, owing to their necessary distance from the observer; and as this distance permits a multitude of local phenomena capable of influencing colour, such as accidental sunbeams, refractions, transparencies, or local mists and showers, to be collected into a space apparently small, the colours of these clouds are always changeful and palpitating; and whatever degree of grey or of gloom may be mixed with them is invariably pure and aerial. But the nearness of the rain-cloud rendering it impossible for a number of phenomena to be at once visible, makes its hue of grey monotonous, and (by losing the blue of distance) warm and brown compared with that of the upper clouds. This is especially remarkable on any part of it which may happen to be illumined, such part being of a brown, bricky, ochreous tone, never bright, always coming in dark outline on the lights of the central clouds. But it is seldom that this takes place, and when it does, never over large spaces, little being usually seen of the rain-cloud but its under and dark side. This, when the cloud above is dense, becomes of an inky and cold grey, and sulphurous and lurid if there be thunder in the air.

With these striking differences in colour, it presents no fewer nor less important in form, chiefly from losing almost all definiteness of character and outline. It is sometimes nothing more than a thin mist, whose outline cannot be traced, rendering the landscape locally indistinct or dark; if its outline be visible, it is ragged and torn, rather a spray of cloud, taken off its edge and sifted by the wind, than an edge of the cloud itself. In fact, it rather partakes of the nature, and assumes the appearance, of real water in the state of spray, than of elastic vapour. This appearance is enhanced by the usual presence of formed rain, carried along with it in a columnar form, ordinarily of course reaching the ground like a veil, but very often suspended with the cloud, and hanging from it like a jagged fringe, or over it, in light, rain being always lighter than the cloud it falls from. These columns or fringes of rain are often waved and bent by the wind, or twisted, sometimes even swept upwards from the clouds. The velocity of these vapours, though not necessarily in reality greater than that of the central clouds, appears greater, owing to their proximity, and, of course, also to the usual presence of a more violent wind. They are also apparently much more in the power of the wind, having less elastic force in themselves; but they are precisely subject to the same great laws of form which regulate the upper clouds. They are not solid bodies borne about with the wind, but they carry the wind with them, and cause it. Everyone knows, who has ever been out in a storm, that the time when it rains heaviest is precisely the time when he cannot hold up his umbrella; that the wind is carried with the cloud, and lulls when it has passed. Everyone who has ever seen rain in a hill country knows that a rain-cloud, like any other, may have all its parts in rapid motion, and yet, as a whole, remain in one spot. I remember once, when in crossing the Tête Noire, I had turned up the valley towards Trient, I noticed a rain-cloud forming on the Glacier de Trient. With a west wind, it proceeded towards the Col de Balme, being followed by a prolonged wreath of vapour always forming exactly at the same spot over the glacier. This long, serpent-like line of cloud went on at a great rate till it reached the valley leading down from the Col de Balme, under the slate rocks of the Croix de Fer. There it turned sharp round, and came down this valley, at right angles to its former progress, and finally directly contrary to it, till it came down within 500 feet of the village, where it disappeared; the line behind always advancing, and always disappearing, at the same spot. This continued for half an hour, the long line describing the curve of a horse-shoe; always coming into existence and always vanishing at exactly the same places; traversing the space between with enormous swiftness. This cloud, ten miles off, would have looked like a perfectly motionless wreath, in the form of a horse-shoe, hanging over the hills.

To the region of the rain-cloud belong also the phenomena of drifted smoke, heat-haze, local mists in the morning or evening, in valleys or over water, mirage, white steaming vapour rising in evaporation from moist and open surfaces, and everything which visibly affects the condition of the atmosphere without actually assuming the form of a cloud. These phenomena are as perpetual in all countries as they are beautiful, and afford by far the most effective and valuable means which the painter possesses, for modification of the forms of fixed objects. The upper clouds are distinct and comparatively opaque, they do not modify, but conceal; but, through the rain-cloud and its accessory phenomena, all that is beautiful may be made manifest, and all that is hurtful concealed; what is paltry may be made to look vast; and what is ponderous, aerial; mystery may be obtained without obscurity, and decoration without disguise. And, accordingly, Nature herself uses it constantly, as one of her chief means of most perfect effect; not in one country, nor another, but wherever there is anything worth calling a landscape. I cannot answer for the desert of Sahara, but I know that there cannot be a greater mistake than supposing that delicate and variable effects of mist and rain-cloud are peculiar to northern climates. I have never seen, in any place or country, effects of mists more perfect than in the Campagna of Rome, and among the hills of Sorrento. It is therefore matter of no little marvel to me, and I conceive that it can scarcely be otherwise to any reflecting person, that throughout the whole range of ancient landscape art there occurs no instance of the painting of a real rain-cloud, still less of any of the more delicate phenomena characteristic of the region. 'Storms' indeed, as the innocent public persist in calling such abuses of Nature and abortions of art as the two windy Gaspars in our National Gallery, are common enough; massive concretions of ink and indigo, wrung and twisted very hard, apparently in a vain effort to get some moisture out of them; bearing up courageously and successfully against a wind whose effects on the trees in the foreground can be accounted for only on the supposition that they are all of the india-rubber species. Enough of this, in all conscience, we have, and to spare; but for the legitimate rain-cloud, with its ragged and spray-like edge, its veilly transparency, and its columnar burden of blessing, neither it, nor anything like it or approaching it, occurs in any painting of the old masters that I have ever seen; and I have seen enough to warrant my affirming that if it occur anywhere, it must be through accident rather than intention. Nor is there stronger evidence of any perception, on the part of these much respected artists, that there were such things in the world as mists or vapours. If a cloud under their direction ever touches a mountain, it does it effectually and as if it meant to do it.

There is no mystifying the matter; here is a cloud, and there is a hill; if it is to come on at all, it comes on to some purpose, and there is no hope of its ever going off again. We have, therefore, little to say of the efforts of the old masters, in any scenes which might naturally have been connected with the clouds of the lowest region, except that the faults of form specified in considering the central clouds are, by way of being energetic or sublime, more glaringly and audaciously committed in their 'storms'; and that what is wrong form among clouds possessing form, is there given with increased generosity of fiction to clouds which have no form at all.

. . . The conclusion, then, to which we are led by our present examination of the truth of clouds is, that the old masters attempted the representation of only one among the thousands of their systems of scenery, and were altogether false in the little they attempted; while we can find records in modern art of every form or phenomenon of the heavens from the highest film that glorifies the ether to the wildest vapour that darkens the dust, and in all these records, we find the most clear language and close thought, firm words and true message, unstinted fullness and unfailing faith.

And indeed it is difficult for us to conceive how, even without such laborious investigation as we have gone through, any person can go to Nature for a single day or hour, when she is really at work in any of her nobler spheres of action, and yet retain respect for the old masters; finding, as find he will, that every scene which rises, rests, or departs before him, bears with it a thousand glories of which there is not one shadow, one image, one trace or line, in any one of their works; but which will illustrate to him, at every new instant, some passage which he had not before understood in the high works of modern art. Stand upon the peak of some isolated mountain at daybreak, when the night mists first rise from off the plains, and watch their white and lake-like fields, as they float in level bays and winding gulfs about the islanded summits of the lower hills, untouched yet by more than dawn, colder and more quiet than a windless sea under the moon of midnight; watch when the first sunbeam is sent upon the silver channels, how the foam of their undulating surface parts and passes away, and down under their depths the glittering city and green pasture lie like Atlantis, between the white paths of winding rivers; the flakes of light falling every moment faster and broader among the starry spires; as the wreathed surges break and vanish above them, and the confused crests and ridges of the dark hills shorten their grey shadows upon the plain. Has Claude given this? Wait a little longer, and you shall see those scattered mists rallying in the ravines, and floating up towards you, along the winding valleys, till they couch in quiet masses, iridescent with the morning light, until they fade away, lost in its lustre, to appear again above, in the serene heaven, like a wild, bright, impossible dream, foundationless and inaccessible, their very bases vanishing in the unsubstantial and mocking blue of the deep lake below. Has Claude given this? Wait yet a little longer, and you shall see those mists gather themselves into white towers, and stand like fortresses along the promontories, massy and motionless, only piled with every instant higher and higher into the sky, and casting longer shadows athwart the rocks; and out of the pale blue of the horizon you will see forming and advancing a troop of narrow, dark, pointed vapours, which will cover the sky, inch by inch, with their grey network, and take the light off the landscape with an eclipse which will stop the singing of the birds and the motion of the leaves, together; and then you will see horizontal bars of black shadow forming under them, and lurid wreaths create themselves, you know not how, along the shoulders of the hills; you never see them form, but when you look back to a place which was clear an instant ago, there is a cloud on it, hanging by the precipices, as a hawk pauses over his prey. Has Claude given this? And then you will hear the sudden rush of the awakened wind, and you will see those watch-towers of vapour swept away from their foundations, and waving curtains of opaque rain let down to the valleys, swinging from the burdened clouds in black bending fringes, or pacing in pale columns along the lake level, grazing its surface into foam as they go. And then, as the sun sinks, you shall see the storm drift for an instant from off the hills, leaving their broad sides smoking, and loaded yet with snow-white, torn, steam-like rags of capricious vapour, now gone, now gathered again; while the smouldering sun, seeming not far away, but burning like a red-hot ball beside you, and as if you could reach it, plunges through the rushing wind and rolling cloud with headlong fall, as if it meant to rise no more, dyeing all the air about it with blood. Has Claude given this? And then you shall hear the fainting tempest die in the hollow of the night, and you shall see a green halo kindling on the summit of the eastern hills, brighter—brighter yet, till the large white circle of the slow moon is lifted up among the barred clouds, step by step, line by line; star after star she quenches with her kindling light setting in their stead an army of pale, penetrable, fleecy wreaths in the heaven, to give light upon the earth, which move together, hand in hand, company by company, troop by troop, so measured in their unity of motion, that the whole heaven seems to roll with them, and the earth to reel under them. Ask Claude, or his brethren, for that. And then wait yet for one hour, until the east again becomes purple, and the heaving mountains, rolling against it in darkness, like waves of a wild sea, are drowned one by one in the glory of its burning: watch the white glaciers blaze in their winding paths about the mountains, like mighty serpents with scales of fire: watch the columnar peaks of solitary snow, kindling downwards, chasm by chasm, each in itself a new morning; their long avalanches cast down in keen streams brighter than the lightning; sending each his tribute of driven snow, like altar-smoke, up to the heaven; the rose-light of their silent domes flushing that heaven about them and above them, piercing with purer light through its purple lines of lifted cloud, casting a new glory on every wreath as it passes by, until the whole heaven, one scarlet canopy, is interwoven with a roof of waving flame, and tossing, vault beyond vault, as with the drifted wings of many companies of angels; and then, when you can look no more for gladness, and when you are bowed down with fear and love of the Maker and Doer of this, tell me who has best delivered this His message unto men!

From *Modern Painters*

OF IMAGINATION PENETRATIVE
[ANGELICO AND TINTORETTO
CONTRASTED]

LET US TAKE ANOTHER INSTANCE. NO SUBJECT HAS BEEN more frequently or exquisitely treated by the religious painters than that of the Annunciation; though, as usual, the most perfect type of its pure ideal has been given by Angelico, and by him with the most radiant consummation (so far as I know) in a small reliquary in the sacristy of Sta. Maria Novella. The background there, however, is altogether decorative; but, in the fresco of the corridor of St. Mark's, the concomitant circumstances are of exceeding loveliness. The Virgin sits in an open loggia, resembling that of the Florentine church of L'Annunziata. Before her is a meadow of rich herbage, covered with daisies. Behind her is seen, through the door at the end of the loggia, a chamber with a single grated window, through which a starlight beam of light falls into the silence. All is exquisite in feeling, but not inventive nor imaginative. Severe would be the shock and painful the contrast, if we could pass in an instant from that pure vision to the wild thought of Tintoret. For not in meek reception of the adoring messenger, but startled by the rush of his horizontal and rattling wings, the Virgin sits, not in the quiet loggia, not by the green pasture of the restored soul, but houseless, under the shelter of a palace vestibule ruined and abandoned, with the noise of the axe and the hammer in her ears, and the tumult of a city round about her desolation. The spectator turns away at first, revolted, from the central object of the picture forced painfully and coarsely forward, a mass of shattered brickwork

C 17

with the plaster mildewed away from it, and the mortar mouldering from its seams; and if he looks again, either at this or at the carpenter's tools beneath it, will perhaps see, in the one and the other, nothing more than such a study of scene as Tintoret could but too easily obtain among the ruins of his own Venice, chosen to give a coarse explanation of the calling and the condition of the husband of Mary. But there is more meant than this. When he looks at the composition of the picture, he will find the whole symmetry of it depending on a narrow line of light, the edge of a carpenter's square, which connects these unused tools with an object at the top of the brickwork, a white stone, four square, the corner-stone of the old edifice, the base of its supporting column. This, I think, sufficiently explains the typical character of the whole. The ruined house is the Jewish dispensation; that obscurely arising in the dawning of the sky is the Christian; but the corner-stone of the old building remains, though the builders' tools lie idle beside it, and the stone which the builders refused is become the Headstone of the Corner.

From *The Stones of Venice*. 1851–1853

ST. MARK'S

.... AND NOW I WISH THAT THE READER, BEFORE I BRING
him into St. Mark's Place, would imagine himself for a little time
in a quiet English cathedral town, and walk with me to the
west front of its cathedral. Let us go together up the more
retired street, at the end of which we can see the pinnacles of
one of the towers, and then through the low grey gateway,
with its battlemented top and small latticed window in the
centre, into the inner private-looking road or close, where
nothing goes in but the carts of the tradesmen who supply the
bishop and the chapter, and where there are little shaven grass-
plots, fenced in by neat rails, before old-fashioned groups of
somewhat diminutive and excessively trim houses, with little
oriel and bay windows jutting out here and there, and deep
wooden cornices and eaves painted cream colour and white,
and small porches to their doors in the shape of cockle-shells,
or little, crooked, thick, indescribable wooden gables warped
a little on one side; and so forward till we come to larger
houses, also old-fashioned, but of red brick, and with garden
behind them, and fruit walls, which show here and there,
among the nectarines, the vestiges of an old cloister arch or
shaft, and looking in front on the cathedral square itself, laid
out in rigid divisions of smooth grass and gravel walk, yet
not uncheerful, especially on the sunny side, where the canons'
children are walking with their nurserymaids. And so, taking
care not to tread on the grass, we will go along the straight
walk to the west front, and there stand for a time, looking
up at its deep-pointed porches and the dark places between
their pillars where there were statues once, and where the

fragments, here and there, of a stately figure are still left, which
has in it the likeness of a king, perhaps indeed a king on earth,
perhaps a saintly king long ago in heaven; and so higher and
higher up to the great mouldering wall of rugged sculpture and
confused arcades, shattered, and grey, and grisly with heads of
dragons and mocking fiends, worn by the rain and swirling
winds into yet unseemlier shape, and coloured on their stony
scales by the deep russet-orange lichen, melancholy gold; and
so, higher still, to the bleak towers, so far above that the eye
loses itself among the bosses of their traceries, though they are
rude and strong, and only sees like a drift of eddying black
points, now closing, now scattering, and now settling suddenly
into invisible places among the bosses and flowers, the crowd
of restless birds that fill the whole square with that strange
clangour of theirs, so harsh and yet so soothing, like the cries
of birds on a solitary coast between the cliffs and sea.

Think for a little while of that scene, and the meaning of
all its small formalisms, mixed with its serene sublimity.
Estimate its secluded, continuous, drowsy felicities, and its
evidence of the sense and steady performance of such kind of
duties as can be regulated by the cathedral clock; and weigh
the influence of those dark towers on all who have passed
through the lonely square at their feet for centuries, and on
all who have seen them rising far away over the wooded plain,
or catching on their square masses the last rays of the sunset,
when the city at their feet was indicated only by the mist at
the bend of the river. And then let us quickly recollect that
we are in Venice, and land at the extremity of the Calle Lunga
San Moisè, which may be considered as there answering to the
secluded street that led us to our English cathedral gateway.

We find ourselves in a paved alley, some seven feet wide
where it is widest, full of people, and resonant with cries of
itinerant salesmen—a shriek in their beginning, and dying away
into a kind of brazen ringing, all the worse for its confinement

between the high houses of the passage along which we have to make our way. Overhead an inextricable confusion of rugged shutters, and iron balconies and chimney flues pushed out on brackets to save room, and arched windows with projecting sills of Istrian stone, and gleams of green leaves here and there where a fig-tree branch escapes over a lower wall from some inner cortile, leading the eye up to the narrow stream of blue sky high over all. On each side, a row of shops, as densely set as may be, occupying, in fact, intervals between the square stone shafts, about eight feet high, which carry the first floors: intervals of which one is narrow and serves as a door; the other is, in the more respectable shops, wainscotted to the height of the counter and glazed above, but in those of the poorer tradesmen left open to the ground, and the wares laid on benches and tables in the open air, the light in all cases entering at the front only, and fading away in a few feet from the threshold into a gloom which the eye from without cannot penetrate, but which is generally broken by a ray or two from a feeble lamp at the back of the shop, suspended before a print of the Virgin. The less pious shopkeeper sometimes leaves his lamp unlighted, and is contented with a penny print; the more religious one has his print coloured and set in a little shrine with a gilded or figured fringe, with perhaps a faded flower or two on each side, and his lamp burning brilliantly. Here at the fruiterer's, where the dark-green water-melons are heaped upon the counter like cannon balls, the Madonna has a tabernacle of fresh laurel leaves; but the pewterer next door has let his lamp out, and there is nothing to be seen in his shop but the dull gleam of the studded patterns on the copper pans, hanging from his roof in the darkness. Next comes a *Vendita Frittole e Liquori*, where the Virgin, enthroned in a very humble manner beside a tallow candle on a back shelf, presides over certain ambrosial morsels of a nature too ambiguous to be defined or enumerated. But a few steps farther on, at the regular wine-shop of the calle, where we are offered *Vino Nostrani a Soldi 28.32*, the Madonna is in great glory, enthroned above ten or a dozen large red casks of three-year-old vintage, and flanked by goodly ranks of bottles of Maraschino, and two crimson lamps; and for the evening, when the gondoliers will come to drink out, under her auspices, the money they have gained during the day, she will have a whole chandelier.

A yard or two farther, we pass the hostelry of the Black Eagle, and glancing as we pass through the square door of marble, deeply moulded, in the outer wall, we see the shadows of its pergola of vines resting on an ancient well, with a pointed shield carved on its side; and so presently emerge on the bridge and Campo San Moisè, whence to the entrance into St. Mark's Place, called the *Bocca di Piazza* (mouth of the square), the Venetian character is nearly destroyed, first by the frightful façade of San Moisè, which we will pause at another time to examine, and then by the modernizing of the shops as they near the piazza, and the mingling with the lower Venetian populace of lounging groups of English and Austrians. We will push fast through them into the shadow of the pillars at the end of the *Bocca di Piazza*, and then we forget them all; for between those pillars there opens a great light, and, in the midst of it, as we advance slowly, the vast tower of St. Mark seems to lift itself visibly forth from the level field of chequered stones; and, on each side, the countless arches prolong themselves into ranged symmetry, as if the rugged and irregular houses that pressed together above us in the dark alley had been struck back into sudden obedience and lovely order, and all their rude casements and broken walls had been transformed into arches charged with goodly sculpture, and fluted shafts of delicate stone.

And well may they fall back, for beyond those troops of ordered arches there rises a vision out of the earth, and all the great square seems to have opened from it in a kind of awe, that we may see it far away; a multitude of pillars and white domes, clustered into a long low pyramid of coloured light; a treasure-heap, it seems, partly of gold, and partly of opal and mother-of-pearl, hollowed beneath into five great vaulted porches, ceiled with fair mosaic, and beset with sculpture of alabaster, clear as amber and delicate as ivory—sculpture fantastic and involved, of palm leaves and lilies, and grapes and pomegranates, and birds clinging and fluttering among the branches, all twined together into an endless network of buds and plumes; and in the midst of it, the solemn forms of angels, sceptred, and robed to the feet, and leaning to each other across the gates, their figures indistinct among the gleaming of the golden ground through the leaves beside them, interrupted and dim, like the morning light as it faded back among the branches of Eden, when first its gates were angel-guarded long ago. And round the walls of the porches there are set pillars of variegated stones, jasper and porphyry, and deep-green serpentine spotted with flakes of snow, and marbles, that half refuse and half yield to the sunshine, Cleopatra-like, 'their bluest veins to kiss'—the shadow, as it steals back from them, revealing line after line of azure undulation, as a receding tide leaves the waved sand; their capitals rich with interwoven tracery, rooted knots of herbage, and drifting leaves of acanthus and vine, and mystical signs, all beginning and ending in the Cross; and above them, in the broad archivolts, a continuous chain of language and of life—angels, and the signs of heaven, and the labours of men, each in its appointed season upon the earth; and above these, another range of glittering pinnacles, mixed with white arches edged with scarlet flowers—a confusion of delight, amidst which the breasts of the Greek horses are seen blazing in their breadth of golden strength, and the St. Mark's lion, lifted on a blue field covered with stars, until at last, as if in ecstasy, the crests of the arches break into a marble foam, and toss themselves far into the blue sky in flashes and wreaths of sculptured spray, as if the breakers on the Lido shore had been frostbound before they fell, and the sea-nymphs had inlaid them with coral and amethyst.

Between that grim cathedral of England and this, what an interval! There is a type of it in the very birds that haunt them; for, instead of the restless crowd, hoarse-voiced and sable-winged, drifting on the bleak upper air, the St. Mark's porches are full of doves, that nestle among the marble foliage, and mingle the soft iridescence of their living plumes, changing at every motion, with the tints, hardly less lovely, that have stood unchanged for 700 years.

And what effect has this splendour on those who pass beneath it? You may walk from sunrise to sunset, to and fro, before the gateway of St. Mark's, and you will not see an eye lifted to it, nor a countenance brightened by it. Priest and layman, soldier and civilian, rich and poor, pass by it alike regardlessly. Up to the very recesses of the porches, the meanest tradesmen of the city push their counters; nay, the foundations of its pillars are themselves the seats—not 'of them that sell doves' for sacrifice, but of the vendors of toys and caricatures. Round the whole square in front of the church there is almost a continuous line of cafés, where the idle Venetians of the middle classes lounge, and read empty journals; in its centre the Austrian bands play during the time of vespers, their martial music jarring with the organ notes—the march drowning the miserere, and the sullen crowd thickening round them—a crowd, which, if it had its will, would stiletto every soldier that pipes to it. And in the recesses of the porches, all day long, knots of men of the lowest classes, unemployed and listless, lie basking in the sun like lizards; and unregarded children—every heavy glance of their young eyes full of desperation and stony depravity, and their throats hoarse with cursing—gamble, and fight, and snarl, and sleep, hour after hour, clashing their bruised centesimi upon the marble ledges of the church porch. And the images of Christ and His angels look down upon it continually.

That we may not enter the church out of the midst of the horror of this, let us turn aside under the portico which looks towards the sea, and passing round within the two massive pillars brought from St. Jean d'Acre, we shall find the gate of the Baptistery; let us enter there. The heavy door closes behind us instantly, and the light and the turbulence of the Piazzetta are together shut out by it.

We are in a low vaulted room; vaulted, not with arches but with small cupolas starred with gold, and chequered with gloomy figures: in the centre is a bronze font charged with rich bas-reliefs, a small figure of the Baptist standing above it in a single ray of light that glances across the narrow room, dying as it falls from a window high in the wall, and the first thing that it strikes, and the only thing that it strikes brightly, is a tomb. We hardly know if it be a tomb indeed; for it is like a narrow couch set beside the window, low-roofed and curtained, so that it might seem, but that it is some height above the pavement, to have been drawn towards the window, that the sleeper might be awakened early; only there are two angels, who have drawn the curtain back, and are looking down upon him. Let us look also, and thank that gentle light that rests upon his forehead for ever, and dies away upon his breast.

The face is of a man in middle life, but there are two deep furrows right across the forehead, dividing it like the foundations of a tower: the height of it above is bound by the fillet of the ducal cap. The rest of the features are singularly small and delicate, the lips sharp, perhaps the sharpness of death being added to that of the natural lines; but there is a sweet smile upon them, and a deep serenity upon the whole countenance. The roof of the canopy above has been blue, filled with stars; beneath, in the centre of the tomb on which the figure rests, is a seated figure of the Virgin, and the border of it all around is of flowers and soft leaves, growing rich and deep, as if in a field in summer.

It is the Doge Andrea Dandolo, a man early great among the great of Venice; and early lost. She chose him for her king in his thirty-sixth year; he died ten years later, leaving behind him that history to which we owe half of what we know of her former fortunes.

Look round at the room in which he lies. The floor of it is of rich mosaic, encompassed by a low seat of red marble, and its walls are of alabaster, but worn and shattered, and darkly stained with age, almost a ruin—in places the slabs of marble have fallen away altogether, and the rugged brickwork is seen through the rents, but all beautiful; the ravaging fissures fretting their way among the islands and channelled zones of the alabaster, and the time-stains on its translucent masses darkened into fields of rich golden brown, like the colour of seaweed when the sun strikes on it through deep sea. The light fades away into the recess of the chamber towards the altar, and the eye can hardly trace the lines of the bas-relief behind it of the baptism of Christ: but on the vaulting of the roof the figures are distinct, and there are seen upon it two great circles, one surrounded by the 'Principalities and powers in heavenly places', of which Milton has expressed the ancient division in the single massy line,

Thrones, Dominations, Princedoms, Virtues, Powers

and around the other, the Apostles; Christ the centre of both and upon the walls, again and again repeated, the gaunt figure of the Baptist, in every circumstance of his life and death; and the streams of the Jordan running down between their cloven rocks; the axe laid to the root of a fruitless tree that springs up on their shore. 'Every tree that bringeth not forth good fruit shall be hewn down, and cast into the fire.' Yes, verily:

to be baptized with fire, or to be cast therein; it is the choice set before all men. The march-notes still murmur through the grated window, and mingle with the sounding in our ears of the sentence of judgment, which the old Greek has written on that Baptistery wall. Venice has made her choice.

He who lies under that stony canopy would have taught her another choice, in his day, if she would have listened to him; but he and his counsels have long been forgotten by her, and the dust lies upon his lips.

Through the heavy door whose bronze network closes the place of his rest, let us enter the church itself. It is lost in still deeper twilight, to which the eye must be accustomed for some moments before the form of the building can be traced; and then there opens before us a vast cave, hewn out into the form of a Cross, and divided into shadowy aisles by many pillars. Round the domes of its roof the light enters only through narrow apertures like large stars; and here and there a ray or two from some far-away casement wanders into the darkness, and casts a narrow phosphoric stream upon the waves of marble that heave and fall in a thousand colours along the floor. What else there is of light is from torches, or silver lamps, burning ceaselessly in the recesses of the chapels; the roof sheeted with gold, and the polished walls covered with alabaster, give back at every curve and angle some feeble gleaming to the flames; and the glories round the heads of the sculptured saints flash out upon us as we pass them, and sink again into the gloom. Under foot and over head, a continual succession of crowded imagery, one picture passing into another, as in a dream; forms beautiful and terrible mixed together; dragons and serpents, and ravening beasts of prey, and graceful birds that in the midst of them drink from running fountains and feed from vases of crystal; the passions and the pleasures of human life symbolized together; and the mystery of its redemption; for the mazes of interwoven lines

and changeful pictures lead always at last to the Cross, lifted
and carved in every place and upon every stone; sometimes
with the serpent of eternity wrapt round it, sometimes with
doves beneath its arms, and sweet herbage growing forth from
its feet; but conspicuous most of all on the great rood that
crosses the church before the altar, raised in bright blazonry
against the shadow of the apse. And although in the recesses
of the aisles and chapels, when the mist of the incense hangs
heavily, we may see continually a figure traced in faint lines
upon their marble, a woman standing with her eyes raised to
heaven, and the inscription above her, 'Mother of God', she
is not here the presiding deity. It is the Cross that is first seen,
and always burning in the centre of the temple; and every
dome and hollow of its roof has the figure of Christ in the
utmost height of it, raised in power, or returning in judgment.

Nor is this interior without effect on the minds of the people.
At every hour of the day there are groups collected before the
various shrines, and solitary worshippers scattered through the
darker places of the church, evidently in prayer both deep and
reverent, and, for the most part, profoundly sorrowful. The
devotees at the greater number of the renowned shrines of
Romanism may be seen murmuring their appointed prayers
with wandering eyes and unengaged gestures; but the step of
the stranger does not disturb those who kneel on the pavement
of St. Mark's; and hardly a moment passes, from early morning
to sunset, in which we may not see some half-veiled figure
enter beneath the Arabian porch, cast itself into long abasement
on the floor of the temple, and then rising slowly with more
confirmed step, and with a passionate kiss and clasp of the arms
given to the feet of the crucifix, by which the lamps burn
always in the northern aisle, leave the church, as if comforted.

But we must not hastily conclude from this that the nobler
characters of the building have at present any influence in
fostering a devotional spirit. There is distress enough in

Venice to bring many to their knees, without excitement from external imagery; and whatever there may be in the temper of the worship offered in St. Mark's more than can be accounted for by reference to the unhappy circumstances of the city, is assuredly not owing either to the beauty of its architecture or to the impressiveness of the Scripture histories embodied in its mosaics. That it has a peculiar effect, however slight, on the popular mind, may perhaps be safely conjectured from the number of worshippers which it attracts, while the churches of St. Paul and the Frari, larger in size and more central in position, are left comparatively empty.[1] But this effect is altogether to be ascribed to its richer assemblage of those sources of influence which address themselves to the commonest instincts of the human mind, and which, in all ages and countries, have been more or less employed in the support of superstition. Darkness and mystery; confused recesses of building; artificial light employed in small quantity, but maintained with a constancy which seems to give it a kind of sacredness; preciousness of material easily comprehended by the vulgar eye; close air loaded with a sweet and peculiar odour associated only with religious services, solemn music, and tangible idols or images having popular legends attached to them—these, the stage properties of superstition, which have been from the beginning of the world, and must be to the end of it, employed by all nations, whether openly savage or nominally civilized, to produce a false awe in minds incapable of apprehending the true nature of the Deity, are assembled in St. Mark's to a degree, as far as I know, unexampled in any other European church. The arts of the Magus and the Brahmin are exhausted in the animation of a paralysed Christianity;

[1] The mere warmth of St. Mark's in winter, which is much greater than that of the other two churches above named, must, however, be taken into consideration, as one of the most efficient causes of its being then more frequented.

and the popular sentiment which these arts excite is to be regarded by us with no more respect than we should have considered ourselves justified in rendering to the devotion of the worshippers at Eleusis, Ellors, or Edfou.[1]

[1] I said above that the larger number of the devotees entered by the 'Arabian' porch; the porch, that is to say, on the north side of the church, remarkable for its rich Arabian archivolt, and through which access is gained immediately to the northern transept. The reason is, that in that transept is the chapel of the Madonna, which has a greater attraction for the Venetians than all the rest of the church besides. The old builders kept their images of the Virgin subordinate to those of Christ; but modern Romanism has retrograded from theirs, and the most glittering portions of the whole church are the two recesses behind this lateral altar, covered with silver hearts dedicated to the Virgin.

From *The Stones of Venice*

THE NATURE OF GOTHIC

SAVAGENESS. I AM NOT SURE WHEN THE WORD 'GOTHIC' was first generically applied to the architecture of the north; but I presume that, whatever the date of its original usage, it was intended to imply reproach, and express the barbaric character of the nations among whom that architecture arose. It never implied that they were literally of Gothic lineage, far less that their architecture had been originally invented by the Goths themselves; but it did imply that they and their buildings together exhibited a degree of sternness and rudeness, which, in contradistinction to the character of southern and eastern nations, appeared like a perpetual reflection of the contrast between the Goth and the Roman in their first encounter. And when that fallen Roman, in the utmost impotence of his luxury, and insolence of his guilt, became the model for the imitation of civilized Europe, at the close of the so-called Dark Ages, the word Gothic became a term of unmitigated contempt, not unmixed with aversion. From that contempt, by the exertion of the antiquaries and architects of this century, Gothic architecture has been sufficiently vindicated; and perhaps some among us, in our admiration of the magnificent science of its structure, and sacredness of its expression, might desire that the term of ancient reproach should be withdrawn, and some other, of more apparent honourableness, adopted in its place. There is no chance, as there is no need, of such a substitution. As far as the epithet was used scornfully, it was used falsely; but there is no reproach in the word, rightly understood; on the contrary, there is a profound truth, which the instinct of mankind almost unconsciously recognizes. It

31

is true, greatly and deeply true, that the architecture of the
north is rude and wild; but it is not true, that, for this reason,
we are to condemn it, or despise. Far otherwise: I believe it is
in this very character that it deserves our profoundest reverence.

The charts of the world which have been drawn up by
modern science have thrown into a narrow space the expression of a vast amount of knowledge, but I have never yet
seen any one pictorial enough to enable the spectator to
imagine the kind of contrast in physical character which
exists between northern and southern countries. We know
the differences in detail, but we have not that broad glance and
grasp which would enable us to feel them in their fullness.
We know that gentians grow on the Alps, and olives on the
Apennines; but we do not enough conceive for ourselves that
variegated mosaic of the world's surface which a bird sees in
its migration, that difference between the district of the gentian
and of the olive which the stork and the swallow see far off,
as they lean upon the sirocco wind. Let us, for a moment, try
to raise ourselves even above the level of their flight, and
imagine the Mediterranean lying beneath us like an irregular
lake, and all its ancient promontories sleeping in the sun: here
and there an angry spot of thunder, a grey stain of storm,
moving upon the burning field; and here and there a fixed
wreath of white volcano smoke, surrounded by its circle of
ashes; but for the most part a great peacefulness of light,
Syria and Greece, Italy and Spain, laid like pieces of a golden
pavement into the sea-blue, chased, as we stoop nearer to
them, with bossy beaten work of mountain chains, and glowing softly with terraced gardens, and flowers heavy with
frankincense, mixed among masses of laurel, and orange, and
plumy palm, that abate with their grey-green shadows the
burning of the marble rocks, and of the ledges of porphyry,
sloping under lucent sand. Then let us pass farther towards the
north, until we see the orient colours change gradually into

a vast belt of rainy green, where the pastures of Switzerland, and poplar valleys of France, and dark forests of the Danube and Carpathians stretch from the mouths of the Loire to those of the Volga, seen through clefts in grey swirls of rain-cloud and flaky veils of the mist of the brooks, spreading low along the pasture lands: and then, farther north still, to see the earth heave into mighty masses of leaden rock and heathy moor, bordering with a broad waste of gloomy purple that belt of field and wood, and splintering into irregular and grisly islands amidst the northern seas, beaten by storm, and chilled by ice-drift, and tormented by furious pulses of contending tide, until the roots of the last forests fail from among the hill ravines, and the hunger of the north wind bites their peaks into barrenness; and, at last, the wall of ice, durable like iron, sets, deathlike, its white teeth against us out of the polar twilight. And, having once traversed in thought this gradation of the zoned iris of the earth in all its material vastness, let us go down nearer to it, and watch the parallel change in the belt of animal life; the multitudes of swift and brilliant creatures that glance in the air and sea, or tread the sands of the southern zone; striped zebras and spotted leopards, glistening serpents, and birds arrayed in purple and scarlet. Let us contrast their delicacy and brilliancy of colour, and swiftness of motion, with the frost-cramped strength, and shaggy covering, and dusky plumage of the northern tribes; contrast the Arabian horse with the Shetland, the tiger and leopard with the wolf and bear, the antelope with the elk, the bird of paradise with the osprey: and then, submissively acknowledging the great laws by which the earth and all that it bears are ruled throughout their being, let us not condemn, but rejoice in the expression by man of his own rest in the statutes of the lands that gave him birth. Let us watch him with reverence as he sets side by side the burning gems, and smooths with soft sculpture the jasper pillars, that are to reflect a ceaseless sunshine, and

D

rise into a cloudless sky: but not with less reverence let us stand by him, when, with rough strength and hurried stroke, he smites an uncouth animation out of the rocks which he has torn from among the moss of the moorland, and heaves into the darkened air the pile of iron buttress and rugged wall, instinct with a work of an imagination as wild and wayward as the northern sea; creations of ungainly shape and rigid limb, but full of wolfish life; fierce as the winds that beat, and changeful as the clouds that shade them.

There is, I repeat, no degradation, no reproach in this, but all dignity and honourableness: and we should err grievously in refusing either to recognize as an essential character of the existing architecture of the north, or to admit as a desirable character in that which it yet may be, this wildness of thought, and roughness of work, this look of mountain brotherhood between the cathedral and the Alp; this magnificence of sturdy power, put forth only the more energetically because the fine finger-touch was chilled away by the frosty wind, and the eye dimmed by the moor-mist, or blinded by the hail; this out-speaking of the strong spirit of men who may not gather redundant fruitage from the earth, nor bask in dreamy benignity of sunshine, but must break the rock for bread, and cleave the forest for fire, and show, even in what they did for their delight, some of the hard habits of the arm and heart that grew on them as they swung the axe or pressed the plough.

VARIETY

The variety of the Gothic schools is the more healthy and beautiful, because in many cases it is entirely unstudied, and results, not from mere love of change, but from practical necessities. For in one point of view Gothic is not only the best, but the *only rational* architecture, as being that which can fit itself most easily to all services, vulgar or noble. Undefined in its slope of roof, height of shaft, breadth of arch, or disposition of ground plan, it can shrink into a turret, expand into a hall, coil into a staircase, or spring into a spire, with undegraded grace and unexhausted energy; and whenever it finds occasion for change in its form or purpose, it submits to it without the slightest sense of loss either to its unity or majesty—subtle and flexible like a fiery serpent, but ever attentive to the voice of the charmer. And it is one of the chief virtues of the Gothic builders, that they never suffered ideas of outside symmetries and consistencies to interfere with the real use and value of what they did. If they wanted a window, they opened one; a room, they added one; a buttress, they built one; utterly regardless of any established conventionalities of external appearance, knowing (as indeed it always happened) that such daring interruptions of the formal plan would rather give additional interest to its symmetry than injure it. So that, in the best times of Gothic, a useless window would rather have been opened in an unexpected place for the sake of the surprise, than a useful one forbidden for the sake of symmetry. Every successive architect, employed upon a great work, built the pieces he added in his own way, utterly regardless of the style adopted by his predecessors; and if two towers were raised in nominal correspondence at the sides of a cathedral front, one was nearly sure to be different from the other, and in each the style at the top to be different from the style at the bottom.

These marked variations were, however, only permitted as part of the great system of perpetual change which ran through every member of Gothic design, and rendered it as endless a field for the beholder's inquiry as for the builder's imagination: change, which in the best schools is subtle and delicate, and rendered more delightful by intermingling of a noble monotony; in the more barbaric schools is somewhat fantastic and redundant; but, in all, a necessary and constant condition of the life of the school. Sometimes the variety is in one feature, sometimes in another; it may be in the capitals or crockets, in the niches or the traceries, or in all together, but in some way or other of the features it will be found always. If the mouldings are constant, the surface sculpture will change; if the traceries are monotonous, the capitals will change; and if even, as in some fine schools, the early English for example, there is the slightest approximation to an unvarying type of mouldings, capitals, and floral decoration, the variety is found in the disposition of the masses, and in the figure sculpture.

I must now refer for a moment, before we quit the consideration of this, the second mental element of Gothic, to the opening of the third chapter of the *Seven Lamps of Architecture*, in which the distinction was drawn (Section 2) between man gathering and man governing; between his acceptance of the sources of delight from nature, and his development of authoritative or imaginative power in their arrangement: for the two mental elements, not only of Gothic, but of all good architecture, which we have just been examining, belong to it, and are admirable in it, chiefly as it is, more than any other subject of art, the work of man, and the expression of the average power of man. A picture or poem is often little more than a feeble utterance of man's admiration of something out of himself; but architecture approaches more to a creation of his own, born of his necessities, and expressive of his nature. It is also, in some sort, the work of the whole race, while the picture or statue is the work of one only, in most cases more highly gifted than his fellows. And therefore we may expect that the first two elements of good architecture should be expressive of some great truths commonly belonging to the whole race, and necessary to be understood or felt by them in all their work that they do under the sun. And observe what they are:

the confession of Imperfection, and the confession of Desire of Change. The building of the bird and the bee need not express anything like this. It is perfect and unchanging. But just because we are something better than birds or bees, our buildings must confess that we have not reached the perfection we can imagine, and cannot rest in the condition we have attained. If we pretend to have reached either perfection or satisfaction, we have degraded ourselves and our work. God's work only may express that; but ours may never have that sentence written upon it—'And behold, it was very good'. And, observe again, it is not merely as it renders the edifice a book of various knowledge, or a mine of precious thought, that variety is essential to its nobleness. The vital principle is not the love of *Knowledge*, but the love of *Change*. It is the strange *disquietude* of the Gothic spirit that is its greatness; that restlessness of the dreaming mind, that wanders hither and thither among the niches, and flickers feverishly around the pinnacles, and frets and fades in labyrinthine knots and shadows along wall and roof, and yet is not satisfied, nor shall be satisfied. The Greek could stay in his triglyph furrow, and be at peace; but the work of the Gothic art is fretwork still, and it can neither rest in, nor from, its labour, but must pass on, sleeplessly, until its love of change shall be pacified for ever in the change that must come alike on them that wake and them that sleep.

From *The Two Paths*. 1859

THE TWO PATHS

An Address delivered to the Members of the Architectural Association ...

IF WE WERE TO BE ASKED ABRUPTLY, AND REQUIRED TO answer briefly, what qualities chiefly distinguish great artists from feeble artists, we should answer, I suppose, first, their sensibility and tenderness; secondly, their imagination; and thirdly, their industry. Some of us might, perhaps, doubt the justice of attaching so much importance to this last character, because we have all known clever men who were indolent, and dull men who were industrious. But though you may have known clever men who were indolent, you never knew a *great* man who was so; and, during such investigation as I have been able to give to the lives of the artists whose works are in all points noblest, no fact ever looms so large upon me—no law remains so steadfast in the universality of its application—as the fact and law that they are all great workers: nothing concerning them is matter of more astonishment than the quantity they have accomplished in the given length of their life; and when I hear a young man spoken of, as giving promise of high genius, the first question I ask about him is always—Does he work?

But though this quality of industry is essential to an artist, it does not in any wise make an artist; many people are busy, whose doings are little worth. Neither does sensibility make an artist, since, as I hope, many can feel strongly and nobly, who yet care nothing about art. But the gifts which distinctly mark the artist—*without* which he must be feeble in life, forgotten in death—*with* which he may become one of the shakers of the earth, and one of the single lights in heaven—are those of sympathy and imagination. I will not occupy your time, nor incur the risk of your dissent, by endeavouring to give any close definition of this last word. We all have a general and sufficient idea of imagination, and of its work with our hands and in our hearts: we understand it, I suppose, as the imagining or picturing of new things in our thoughts; and we always show an involuntary respect for this power, wherever we can recognize it, acknowledging it to be a greater power than manipulation, or calculation, or observation, or any other human faculty. If we see an old woman spinning at the fireside, and distributing her thread dexterously from the distaff, we respect her for her manipulation—if we ask her how much she expects to make in a year, and she answers quickly, we respect her for her calculation—if she is watching at the same time that none of her grandchildren fall into the fire, we respect her for her observation—yet for all this she may still be a common-place old woman enough. But if she is all the time telling her grandchildren a fairy tale out of her head, we praise her for her imagination, and say, she must be a rather remarkable old woman.

Precisely in like manner, if an architect does his working-drawing well, we praise him for his manipulation—if he keeps closely within his contract, we praise him for his honest arithmetic—if he looks well to the laying of his beams, so that nobody shall drop through the floor, we praise him for his observation. But he must, somehow, tell us a fairy tale out of his head beside all this, else we cannot praise him for his imagination nor speak of him as we did of the old woman, as being in any wise out of the common way, a rather remarkable architect. It seemed to me, therefore, as if it might interest you to-night, if we were to consider together what fairy tales are, in and by architecture, to be told—what there is for you to do in this severe art of yours 'out of your heads', as well as by your hands.

Perhaps the first idea which a young architect is apt to be allured by, as a head-problem in these experimental days, is its being incumbent upon him to invent a 'new style' worthy of modern civilization in general, and of England in particular; a style worthy of our engines and telegraphs; as expansive as steam, and as sparkling as electricity. But, if there are any of my hearers who have been impressed with this sense of inventive duty, may I ask them, first, whether their plan is that every inventive architect amongst us shall invent a new style for himself, and have a county set aside for his conceptions, or a province for his practice? Or, must every architect invent a little piece of the new style, and all put it together at last like a dissected map? And if so, when the new style is invented, what is to be done next? I will grant you this Eldorado of imagination—but can you have more than one Columbus? Or, if you sail in company, and divide the prize of your discovery and the honour thereof, who is to come after your clustered Columbuses? To what fortunate islands of style are your architectural descendants to sail, avaricious of new lands? When our desired style is invented, will not the best we can all do be simply—to build in it?—and cannot you now do that in styles that are known? Observe, I grant, for the sake of your argument, what perhaps many of you know that I would not grant otherwise—that a new style *can* be invented. I grant you not only this, but that it shall be wholly different from any that was ever practised before. We will suppose that capitals are to be at the bottom of pillars instead of at the top; and that buttresses shall be on the tops of pinnacles instead of at the bottom; that you roof your apertures with stones which shall neither be arched nor horizontal; and that you compose your decoration of lines which shall neither be crooked nor straight. The furnace and the forge shall be at your service: you shall draw out your plates of glass and beat out your bars of iron till you have encompassed us all—if your style is of the practical kind—with endless perspective of black skeleton and blinding square—or if your style is to be of the ideal kind—you shall wreathe your streets with ductile leafage, and roof them with variegated crystal— you shall put, if you will, all London under one blazing dome of many colours that shall light the clouds round it with its flashing, as far as to the sea. And still, I ask you, What after this? Do you suppose those imaginations of yours will ever lie down there asleep beneath the shade of your iron leafage, or within the coloured light of your enchanted dome? Not so. Those souls, and fancies, and ambitions of yours, are wholly infinite; and, whatever may be done by others, you will still want to do something for yourselves; if you cannot rest content with Palladio, neither will you with Paxton; all the metal and glass that ever were melted have not so much weight in them as will clog the wings of one human spirit's aspiration.

If you will think over this quietly by yourselves, and can get the noise out of your ears of the perpetual, empty, idle, incomparably idiotic talk about the necessity of some novelty in architecture, you will soon see that the very essence of a Style, properly so called, is that it should be practised *for ages*, and applied to all purposes; and that so long as any given style is in practice, all that is left for individual imagination to accomplish must be within the scope of that style, not in the invention of a new one. If there are any here, therefore, who hope to obtain celebrity by the invention of some strange way of building which must convince all Europe into its adoption, to them, for the moment, I must not be understood to address myself, but only to those who would be content with that degree of celebrity which an artist may enjoy who works in the manner of his forefathers; which the builder of Salisbury Cathedral might enjoy in England, though he did not invent Gothic; and which Titian might enjoy at Venice, though he did not invent oil painting. Addressing myself then to those humbler, but wiser, or rather, only wise students who are content to avail themselves of some system of building already understood, let us consider together what room for the exercise of the imagination may be left to us under such conditions. And, first, I suppose it will be said, or thought, that the architect's principal field for exercise of his invention must be in the disposition of lines, mouldings, and masses, in agreeable proportions. Indeed, if you adopt some styles of architecture, you cannot exercise invention in any other way. And I admit that it requires genius and special gift to do this rightly. Not by rule, nor by study, can the gift of graceful proportionate design be obtained; only by the intuition of genius can so much as a single tier of façade be beautifully arranged; and the man has just cause for pride, as far as our gifts can ever be a cause for pride, who finds himself able, in a design of his own, to rival even the simplest arrangement of parts in one by Sanmicheli, Inigo Jones, or Christopher Wren.

Invention, then, and genius being granted, as necessary to accomplish this, let me ask you, What, after all, with this special gift and genius, you *have* accomplished, when you have arranged the lines of a building beautifully?

In the first place you will not, I think, tell me that the beauty there attained is of a touching or pathetic kind. A well-disposed group of notes in music will make you sometimes weep and sometimes laugh. You can express the depth of all affections by those dispositions of sound; you can give courage to the soldier, language to the lover, consolation to the mourner, more joy to the joyful, more humility to the devout. Can you do as much by your group of lines? Do you suppose the front of Whitehall, a singularly beautiful one, ever inspires the two Horse Guards, during the hour they sit opposite to it, with military ardour? Do you think that the lovers in our London walk down to the front of Whitehall for consolation when mistresses are unkind; or that any person wavering in duty, or feeble in faith, was ever confirmed in purpose or in creed by the pathetic appeal of those harmonious architraves? You will not say so. Then, if they cannot touch, or inspire, or comfort anyone, can your architectural proportions amuse anyone? Christmas is just over; you have doubtless been at many merry parties during the period. Can you remember any in which architectural proportions contributed to the entertainment of the evening? Proportions of notes in music were, I am sure, essential to your amusement; the setting of flowers in hair, and of ribands on dresses, were also subjects of frequent admiration with you, not inessential to your happiness. Among the juvenile members of your society the proportion of currants in cake, and sugar in comfits, became subjects of acute interest; and, when such proportions were harmonious, motives also of gratitude to cook and to confectioner. But, did you ever see young or old amused by the architrave of the door? Or otherwise interested in the proportions of the room than as they admitted more or fewer friendly faces? Nay, if all the amusement that there is in the best-proportioned architecture of London could be concentrated into one evening, and you were to issue tickets for nothing to this great proportional entertainment; how do you think it would stand between you and the Drury pantomime?

You are, then, remember, granted to be the people of genius—great and admirable; and you devote your lives to your art, but you admit that you cannot comfort anybody, you cannot encourage anybody, you cannot improve anybody, and you cannot amuse anybody. I proceed then further to ask, Can you inform anybody? Many sciences cannot be considered as highly touching or emotional; nay, perhaps not specially amusing; scientific men may sometimes, in these respects, stand on the same ground with you. As far as we can judge by the results of the late war, science helps our soldiers about as much as the front of Whitehall; and at the Christmas parties, the children wanted no geologists to tell them about the behaviour of bears and dragons in Queen Elizabeth's time. Still, your man of science teaches you something; he may be dull at a party, or helpless in a battle, he is not always that; but he can give you, at all events, knowledge of noble facts, and open to you the secrets of the earth and air. Will your architectural proportions do as much? Your genius is granted, and your life is given, and what do you teach us?—Nothing, I believe, from one end of that life to the other, but that two and two make four, and that one is to two as three is to six.

You cannot, then, it is admitted, comfort anyone, serve or amuse anyone, nor teach anyone. Finally, I ask, Can you be of *Use* to anyone? 'Yes,' you reply; 'certainly we are of some use— we architects—in a climate like this, where it always rains.' You are of use, certainly; but, pardon me, only as builders— not as proportionalists. We are not talking of building as a protection, but only of that special work which your genius is to do; not of building substantial and comfortable houses like Mr. Cubitt, but of putting beautiful façades on them like Inigo Jones. And, again, I ask—Are you of use to anyone? Will your proportions of façade heal the sick, or clothe the naked? Supposing you devoted your lives to be merchants, you might reflect at the close of them, how many, fainting for want, you had brought corn to sustain; how many, infected with disease, you had brought balms to heal; how widely, among multitudes of far-away nations, you had scattered the first seeds of national power, and guided the first rays of sacred light. Had you been, in fine, *anything* else in the world *but* architectural designers, you might have been of some use or good to people. Content to be petty tradesmen, you would have saved the time of mankind; rough-handed daily labourers, you would have added to their stock of food or of clothing. But, being men of genius, and devoting your lives to the exquisite exposition of this genius, on what achievements do you think the memories of your old age are to fasten? Whose gratitude will surround you with its glow, or on what accomplished good, of that greatest kind for which men show *no* gratitude, will your life rest the contentment of its close? Truly, I fear that the ghosts of proportionate lines will be thin phantoms at your bedsides—very speechless to you; and that on all the emanations of your high genius you will look back with less delight than you might have done on a cup of cold water given to him who was thirsty, or to a single moment when you had 'prevented with your bread him that fled'.

Do not answer, nor think to answer, that with your great works and great payments of workmen in them, you would do this; I know you would and will, as Builders; but, I repeat, it is not your *building* that I am talking about, but your *brains*; it is your invention and your imagination of whose profit I am speaking. The good done through the building, observe, is done by your employers, not by you—you share in the benefit of it. The good that *you* personally must do is by your designing; and I compare you with musicians who do good by their pathetic composing, not as they do good by employing fiddlers in the orchestra; for it is the public who in reality do that, not the musicians. So clearly keeping to this one question, what good we architects are to do by our genius; and having found that on our proportionate system we can do no good to others, will you tell me, lastly, what good we can do to *ourselves*?

Observe, nearly every other liberal art or profession has some intense pleasure connected with it, irrespective of any good to others. As lawyers, or physicians, or clergymen, you would have the pleasure of investigation, and of historical reading, as part of your work: as men of science you would be rejoicing in curiosity perpetually gratified respecting the laws and facts of Nature: as artists you would have delight in watching the external forms of Nature: as day labourers or petty tradesmen, supposing you to undertake such work with as much intellect as you are going to devote to your designing, you would find continued subjects of interest in the manufacture or the agriculture which you helped to improve; or in the problems of commerce which bore your business. But your architectural designing leads you into no pleasant journeys—into no seeing of lovely things—no discerning of just laws—no warmth of compassion, no humilities of veneration, no progressive state of sight or soul. Our conclusion is—must be—that you will not amuse, nor inform, nor help anybody; you will not amuse, nor better, nor inform yourselves: you will sink into a state in which you can neither show, nor feel, nor see, anything, but that one is to two as three is to six. And in that state what should we call ourselves? Men? I think not. The right name for us would be—numerators and denominators. Vulgar Fractions.

Shall we, then, abandon this theory of the soul of architecture being in proportional lines, and look whether we can find anything better to exert our fancies upon?

May we not, to begin with, accept this great principle—that, as our bodies, to be in health, must be *generally* exercised, so our minds, to be in health, must be *generally* cultivated? You would not call a man healthy who had strong arms but was paralytic in his feet; nor one who could walk well, but had no use of his hands; nor one who could see well, if he could not hear. You would not voluntarily reduce your bodies to any such partially developed state. Much more, then, you would not, if you could help it, reduce your minds to it. Now, your minds are endowed with a vast number of gifts of totally different uses—limbs of mind as it were, which, if you don't exercise, you cripple. One is curiosity; that is a gift, a capacity of pleasure in knowing; which, if you destroy, you make yourselves cold and dull. Another is sympathy; the power of sharing in the feelings of living creatures; which, if you destroy, you make yourselves hard and cruel. Another of your limbs of mind is admiration; the power of enjoying beauty or ingenuity;

which, if you destroy, you make yourselves base and irreverent. Another is wit; or the power of playing with the lights on the many sides of truth; which, if you destroy, you make yourselves gloomy, and less useful and cheering to others than you might be. So that in choosing your way of work it should be your aim, as far as possible, to bring out all these faculties, as far as they exist in you; not one merely, nor another, but all of them. And the way to bring them out, is simply to concern yourselves attentively with the subjects of each faculty. To cultivate sympathy you must be among living creatures, and thinking about them; and to cultivate admiration, you must be among beautiful things and looking at them.

All this sounds much like truism, at least, I hope it does, for then you will surely not refuse to act upon it; and to consider further how, as architects, you are to keep yourselves in contemplation of living creatures and lovely things.

You all probably know the beautiful photographs which have been published within the last year or two of the porches of the Cathedral of Amiens. I hold one of these up to you (merely that you may know what I am talking about, as of course you cannot see the detail at this distance, but you will recognize the subject). Have you ever considered how much sympathy, and how much humour, are developed in filling this single doorway with these sculptures of the history of St. Honoré (and, by the way, considering how often we English are now driving up and down the Rue St. Honoré, we may as well know as much of the saint as the old architect cared to tell us). You know, in all legends of saints who ever were bishops, the first thing you are told of them is that they didn't want to be bishops. So here is St. Honoré, who doesn't want to be a bishop, sitting sulkingly in the corner, he hugs his book with both hands, and won't get up to take his crosier; and here are all the city aldermen of Amiens come to *poke* him up; and all the monks in the town in a great puzzle what they shall do for a bishop if St. Honoré won't be; and here's one of the monks in the opposite corner who is quite cool about it, and thinks they'll get on well enough without St. Honoré—you see that in his face quite perfectly. At last St. Honoré consents to be bishop, and here he sits in a throne, and has his book now grandly on a desk instead of his knees, and he directs one of his village curates how to find relics in a wood; here is the wood, and here is the village curate, and here are the tombs, with the bones of St. Victorien and Gentien in them.

After this St. Honoré performs grand mass, and the miracle occurs of the appearance of a hand blessing the wafer, which occurrence afterwards was painted for the arms of the abbey. Then St. Honoré dies; and here is his tomb with his statue on the top; and miracles are being performed at it—a deaf man having his ear touched, and a blind man groping his way up to the tomb with his dog. Then here is a great procession in honour of the relics of St. Honoré; and under his coffin are some cripples being healed; and the coffin itself is put above the bar which separates the cross from the lower subjects, because the tradition is that the figure on the crucifix of the Church of St. Firmin bowed its head in token of acceptance, as the relics of St. Honoré passed beneath.

Now just consider the amount of sympathy with human nature, and observance of it, shown in this one bas-relief; the sympathy with disputing monks, with puzzled aldermen, with melancholy recluse, with triumphant prelate, with palsy-stricken poverty, with ecclesiastical magnificence, or miracle-working faith. Consider how much intellect was needed in the architect, and how much observance of Nature, before he could give the expression to these rich and quaint fragments of tombs and altars—weave with perfect animation the entangled branches of the forest.

But you will answer me, all this is not architecture at all—it is sculpture. Will you then tell me precisely where the separation exists between one and the other? We will begin at the very beginning. I will show you a piece of what you will certainly admit to be a piece of pure architecture; it is drawn on the back of another photograph, another of those marvellous tympana from Notre Dame, which you call, I suppose, impure. Well, look on this picture, and on this. Don't laugh; you must not laugh, that's very improper of you, this is classical architecture. I have taken it out of the essay on that subject in the *Encyclopaedia Britannica*.

Yet I suppose none of you would think yourselves particularly ingenious architects if you had designed nothing more than this; nay, I will even let you improve it into any grand proportion you choose, and add to it as many windows as you choose; the only thing I insist upon in our specimen of pure architecture is, that there should be no mouldings nor ornaments upon it. And I suspect you don't quite like your architecture so 'pure' as this. We want a few mouldings, you will say—just a few. Those who want mouldings, hold up their hands. We are unanimous, I think. Will you, then, design profiles of these mouldings yourselves, or will you copy them? If you wish to copy them, and to copy them always, of course I leave you at once to your authorities, and your imaginations to their repose. But if you wish to design them yourselves, how do you do it? You draw the profile according to your taste, and you order your mason to cut it. Now, will you tell me the logical difference between drawing the profile of a moulding and giving *that* to be cut, and drawing the folds of the drapery of a statue and giving *those* to be cut? The last is much more difficult to do than the first; but degrees of difficulty constitute no specific difference, and you will not accept it, surely, as a definition of the difference between architecture and sculpture, that 'architecture is doing anything that is easy, and sculpture anything that is difficult'.

It is true, also, that the carved moulding represents nothing,

E   49

and the carved drapery represents something; but you will not, I should think, accept, as an explanation of the difference between architecture and sculpture, this any more than the other, that 'sculpture is art which has meaning, and architecture art which has none'.

Where, then, is your difference? In this perhaps, you will say; that whatever ornaments we can direct ourselves, and get accurately cut to order, we consider architectural. The ornaments that we are obliged to leave to the pleasure of the workman, or the superintendence of some other designer, we consider sculptural, especially if they are more or less extraneous and incrusted—not an essential part of the building.

Accepting this definition, I am compelled to reply, that it is in effect nothing more than an amplification of my first one—that whatever is easy you call architecture, whatever is difficult you call sculpture. For you cannot suppose the arrangement of the place in which the sculpture is to be put is so difficult or so great a part of the design as the sculpture itself. For instance: you all know the pulpit of Niccolo Pisano, in the baptistery at Pisa. It is composed of seven rich *relievi*, surrounded by panel mouldings, and sustained on marble shafts. Do you suppose Niccolo Pisano's reputation—such part of it at least as rests on this pulpit (and much does)—depends on the panel mouldings or on the *relievi*? The panel mouldings are by his hand; he would have disdained to leave even them to a common workman; but do you think he found any difficulty in them, or thought there was any credit in them? Having once done the sculpture, those enclosing lines were mere child's play to him; the determination of the diameter of shafts and height of capitals was an affair of minutes; his *work* was in carving the Crucifixion and the Baptism.

Or, again, do you recollect Orcagna's tabernacle in the church of San Michele, at Florence? That, also, consists of rich and multitudinous bas-reliefs, enclosed in panel mouldings, with shafts of mosaic, and foliated arches sustaining the canopy. Do you think Orcagna, any more than Pisano, if his spirit could rise in the midst of us at this moment, would tell us that he had trusted his fame to the foliation, or had put his soul's pride into the panelling? Not so; he would tell you that his spirit was in the stooping figures that stand around the couch of the dying Virgin.

Or, lastly, do you think the man who designed the procession on the portal of Amiens was the subordinate workman? That there was an architect over *him*, restraining him within certain limits, and ordering of him his bishops at so much a mitre, and his cripples at so much a crutch? Not so. *Here*, on this sculptured shield, rests the Master's hand; *this* is the centre of the Master's thought: from this, and in subordination to this, waved the arch and sprang the pinnacle. Having done this, and being able to give human expression and action to the stone, all the rest—the rib, the niche, the foil, the shaft—were mere toys in his hand and accessories to his conception; and if once you also gain the gift of doing this, if once you can carve one fronton such as you have here, I tell you, you would be able— so far as it depended on your invention—to scatter cathedrals over England as fast as clouds rise from its streams after summer rain.

Nay, but perhaps you answer again, our sculptors at present do not design cathedrals, and could not. No, they could not; but that is merely because we have made architecture so dull that they cannot take any interest in it, and, therefore, do not care to add to their higher knowledge the poor and common knowledge of principles of building. You have thus separated building from sculpture, and you have taken away the power of both; for the sculptor loses nearly as much by never having room for the development of a continuous work, as you do from having reduced your work to a continuity of mechanism. You are essentially, and should always be, the same body of men, admitting only such difference in operation as there is between the work of a painter at different times, who sometimes labours on a small picture, and sometimes on the frescoes of a palace gallery.

This conclusion, then, we arrive at, *must* arrive at; the fact being irrevocably so: that in order to give your imagination and the other powers of your souls full play, you must do as all the great architects of old time did—you must yourselves be your sculptors. Phideas, Michelangelo, Orcagna, Pisano, Giotto —which of these men, do you think, could not use his chisel? You say, 'It is difficult; quite out of your way.' I know it is; nothing that is great is easy; and nothing that is great, so long as you study building without sculpture, can be *in* your way. I want to put it in your way, and you find your way to it. But, on the other hand, do not shrink from the task as if the refined art of perfect sculpture were always required from you. For, though architecture and sculpture are not separate arts, there is an architectural *manner* of sculpture; and it is, in the majority of its applications, a comparatively easy one. Our great mistake at present, in dealing with stone at all, is requiring to have all our work too refined; it is just the same mistake as if we were to require all our book illustrations to be as fine work as Raphael's. John Leech does not sketch so well as Leonardo da Vinci; but do you think that the public could easily spare him; or that he is wrong in bringing out his talent in the way in which it is most effective? Would you advise him, if he asked your advice, to give up his wood-blocks and take to canvas? I know you would not; neither would you tell him, I believe, on the other hand, that, because he could not draw as well as Leonardo, therefore he ought to draw nothing but straight lines with a ruler, and circles with compasses, and no figure-subjects at all. That would be some loss to you; would it not? You would all be vexed if next week's *Punch* had nothing in it but proportionate lines. And yet, do not you see that you are doing precisely the same thing with *your* powers of sculptural design that he would be doing with his powers of pictorial design, if he gave you nothing but such lines? You feel that you cannot carve like Phideas; therefore you will not carve at all, but only draw mouldings; and thus all that intermediate power which is of especial value in modern days—that popular power of expression which is within the attainment of thousands, and would address itself to tens of thousands—is utterly lost to us in stone, though in ink and paper it has become one of the most important engines, and one of the most desired luxuries, of modern civilization.

Here, then, is one part of the subject to which I would especially invite your attention, namely, the distinctive character which may be wisely permitted to belong to architectural sculpture, as distinguished from perfect sculpture on one side, and from mere geometrical decoration on the other.

And first, observe what an indulgence we have in the distance at which most work is to be seen. Supposing we were able to carve eyes and lips with the most exquisite precision, it would all be of no use as soon as the work was put far above the eye; but, on the other hand, as beauties disappear by being far withdrawn, so will faults; and the mystery and confusion which are the natural consequence of distance, while they would often render your best skill but vain, will as often render your worst errors of little consequence; nay, more than this, often a deep cut, or a rude angle, will produce in certain positions an effect of expression both startling and true, which you never hoped for. Not that mere distance will give animation to the work, if it has none in itself; but if it has life at all, the distance will make that life more perceptible and powerful by softening the defects of execution. So that you are placed, as workmen, in this position of singular advantage, that you may give your fancies free play, and strike hard for the expression that you want, knowing that, if you miss it, no one will detect you;

if you at all touch it, Nature herself will help you, and with every changing shadow and basking sunbeam bring forth new phases of your fancy.

But it is not merely this privilege of being imperfect which belongs to architectural sculpture. It has a true privilege of imagination, far excelling all that can be granted to the more finished work, which, for the sake of distinction, I will call—and I don't think we can have a much better term—'furniture sculpture'; sculpture, that is, which can be moved from place to place to furnish rooms.

For observe, to that sculpture the spectator is usually brought in a tranquil or prosaic state of mind; he sees it associated rather with what is sumptuous than sublime, and under circumstances which address themselves more to his comfort than his curiosity. The statue which is to be pathetic, seen between the flashes of footmen's livery round the dining-table, must have strong elements of pathos in itself: and the statue which is to be awful, in the midst of the gossip of the drawing-room, must have the elements of awe wholly in itself. But the spectator is brought to *your* work already in an excited and imaginative mood. He has been impressed by the cathedral wall as it loomed over the low streets, before he looks up to the carving of its porch—and his love of mystery has been touched by the silence and the shadows of the cloister, before he can set himself to decipher the bosses on its vaulting. So that when once he begins to observe your doings, he will ask nothing better from you, nothing kinder from you, than that you would meet this imaginative temper of his half-way; that you would further touch the sense of terror, or satisfy the expectation of things strange, which have been prompted by the mystery or the majesty of the surrounding scene. And thus, your leaving forms more or less undefined, or carrying out your fancies, however extravagant, in grotesqueness of shadow or shape, will be for the most part in accordance with the temper of the observer;

and he is likely, therefore, much more willingly to use his fancy to help your meanings, than his judgment to detect your faults.

Again. Remember that when the imagination and feelings are strongly excited, they will not only bear with strange things but they will *look* into *minute* things with a delight quite unknown in hours of tranquillity. You surely must remember moments of your lives in which, under some strong excitement of feeling, all the details of visible objects presented themselves with a strange intensity and insistence [*sic*], whether you would or no; urging themselves upon the mind, and thrust upon the eye, with a force of fascination which you could not refuse. Now, to a certain extent, the senses get into this state whenever the imagination is strongly excited. Things trivial at other times assume a dignity or significance which we cannot explain; but which is only the more attractive because inexplicable: and the powers of attention, quickened by the feverish excitement, fasten and feed upon the minutest circumstances of detail, and remotest traces of intention. So that what would at other times be felt as more or less mean or extraneous in a work of sculpture and which would assuredly be offensive to the perfect taste in its moments of languor, or of critical judgment, will be grateful, and even sublime, when it meets this frightened inquisitiveness, this fascinated watchfulness, or the roused imagination. And this is all for your advantage; for, in the beginnings of your sculpture, you will assuredly find it easier to imitate minute circumstances of costume or character, than to perfect the anatomy of simple forms or the flow of noble masses; and it will be encouraging to remember that the grace you cannot perfect, and the simplicity you cannot achieve, would be in great part vain, even if you could achieve them, in their appeal to the hasty curiosity of passionate fancy; but that the sympathy which would be refused to your science will be granted to your innocence; and that the mind of the general observer, though wholly unaffected by correctness of anatomy or propriety of gesture, will follow you with fond and pleased concurrence, as you carve the knots of the hair, and the patterns of the vesture.

Further yet. We are to remember that not only do the associated features of the larger architecture tend to excite the strength of fancy, but the architectural laws to which you are obliged to submit your decoration stimulate its *ingenuity*. Every crocket which you are to crest with sculpture—every foliation which you have to fill, presents itself to the spectator's fancy, not only as a pretty thing, but as a *problematic* thing. It contained, he perceives immediately, not only a beauty which you wished to display, but a necessity which you were forced to meet; and the problem, how to occupy such and such a space with organic form in any probable way, or how to turn such a boss or ridge into a conceivable image of life, becomes at once, to him as to you, a matter of amusement as much as of admiration. The ordinary conditions of perfection in form, gesture, or feature, are willingly dispensed with, when the ugly dwarf and ungainly goblin have only to gather themselves into angles, or crouch to carry corbeils; and the want of skill which, in other kinds of work, would have been required for the finishing of the parts, will at once be forgiven here, if you have only disposed ingeniously what you have executed roughly, and atoned for the rudeness of your hands by the quickness of your wits.

Hitherto, however, we have been considering only the circumstances in architecture favourable to the development of the *powers* of imagination. A yet more important point for us seems, to me, the place which it gives to all *objects* of imagination.

For, I suppose, you will not wish me to spend any time in proving that imagination must be vigorous in proportion to the quantity of material which it has to handle; and that, just

as we increase the range of what we see, we increase the richness of what we can imagine. Granting this, consider what a
field is open to your fancy merely in the subject-matter which
architecture admits. Nearly every other art is severely limited
in its subjects—the landscape painter, for instance, gets little
help from the aspects of beautiful humanity; the historical
painter, less, perhaps, than he ought, from the accidents of
wild nature; and the pure sculptor, still less, from the minor
details of common life. But is there anything within range of
sight, or conception, which may not be of use to *you*, or in
which your interest may not be excited with advantage to
your art? From visions of angels, down to the least important
gesture of a child at play, whatever may be conceived of
Divine, or beheld of Human, may be dared or adopted by you;
throughout the kingdom of animal life, no creature is so vast,
or so minute, that you cannot deal with it, or bring it into
service; the lion and the crocodile will crouch about your
shafts; the moth and the bee will sun themselves upon your
flowers; for you, the fawn will leap; for you, the snail be slow;
for you, the dove smooth her bosom, and the hawk spread
her wings toward the south. All the wide world of vegetation
blooms and bends for you; the leaves tremble that you may
bid them be still under the marble snow; the thorn and the
thistle, which the earth casts forth as evil, are to you the
kindliest servants; no dying petal, nor drooping tendril, is so
feeble as to have no help for you; no robed pride of blossom
so kingly, but it will lay aside its purple, to receive at your
hands the pale immortality. Is there anything in common
life too mean—in common things too trivial—to be ennobled
by your touch? As there is nothing in life, so there is nothing
in lifelessness which has not its lesson for you, or its gift; and
when you are tired of watching the strength of the plume, and
the tenderness of the leaf, you may walk down to your rough
rivershore, or into the thickest markets of your thoroughfares;

and there is not a piece of torn cable that will not twine into a perfect moulding; there is not a fragment of castaway matting, or shattered basket-work, that will not work into a chequer or a capital. Yes: and if you gather up the very sand, and break the stone on which you tread, among its fragments of all but invisible shells you will find forms that will take their place, and that proudly, among the starred traceries of your vaulting; and you, who can crown the mountain with its fortress, and the city with its towers, are thus able also to give beauty to ashes, and worthiness to dust.

Now, in that your art presents all this material to you, you have already much to rejoice in. But you have more to rejoice in, because all this is submitted to you, not to be dissected or analysed, but to be sympathized with, and to bring out, therefore, what may be accurately called the moral part of imagination. We saw that, if we kept ourselves among lines only, we should have cause to envy the naturalist, because he was conversant with facts; but you will have little to envy now, if you make yourselves conversant with the feelings that arise out of his facts. For instance, the naturalist, coming upon a block of marble, has to begin considering immediately how far its purple is owing to iron, or its whiteness to magnesia; he breaks his piece of marble, and at the close of his day, has nothing but a little sand in his crucible, and some data added to the theory of the elements. But *you* approach your marble to sympathize with it, and rejoice over its beauty. You cut at it a little indeed, but only to bring out its veins more perfectly; and at the end of your day's work you leave your marble shaft with joy and complacency in its perfectness, as marble. When you have to watch an animal instead of a stone, you differ from the naturalist in the same way. He may, perhaps, if he be an amiable naturalist, take delight in having living creatures round him; still the major part of his work is, or has been, in counting feathers, separating fibres, and analysing structures.

But *your* work is always with the living creature; the thing you have to get at in him is his life, and ways of going about things. It does not matter to you how many cells there are in his bones, or how many filaments in his feathers; what you want is his moral character and way of behaving himself; it is just that which your imagination, if healthy, will first seize— just that which your chisel, if vigorous, will first cut. You must get the storm spirit into your eagles, and the lordliness into your lions, and the tripping fear into your fawns; and in order to do this, you must be in continual sympathy with every fawn of them; and be hand-in-glove with all the lions, and hand-in-claw with all the hawks. And don't fancy that you will occupy mind after mind of utterly countless multitudes, long after you are gone. You have not, like authors, to plead for a hearing, or to fear oblivion. Do but build large enough, and carve boldly enough, and all the world will hear you; they cannot choose but look.

I do not mean to awe you by this thought; I do not mean that, because you will have so many witnesses and watchers, you are never to jest, or do anything gaily or lightly; on the contrary, I have pleaded, from the beginning, for this art of yours, especially because it has room for the whole of your character: if jest is in you, let the jest be jested; if mathematical ingenuity is yours, let your problem be put, and your solution be worked out, as quaintly as you choose; above all, see that your work is easily and happily done, else it will never make anybody else happy; but while you thus give the rein to all your impulses see that those impulses be heeded and centred by one noble impulse; and let that be Love—triple love—for the art which you practise, the creation in which you move, and the creatures to whom you minister.

I say, first, Love for the art which you practise. Be assured that if ever any other motive becomes a leading one in your mind, as the principal one for exertion, except your love of art, that moment it is all over with your art. I do not say you are not to desire money, nor to desire fame, nor to desire position; you cannot but desire all three; nay, you may—if you are willing that I should use the word Love in a desecrated sense—love all three; that is, passionately covet them; yet you must not covet or love them in the first place. Men of strong passions and imaginations must always care a great deal for anything, but the whole question is one of first or second. Does your art lead you, or your gain lead you? You may like making money exceedingly; but if it comes to a fair question, whether you are to make five hundred pounds less by this business, or to spoil your building, and you choose to spoil your building, there's an end of you. So you may be as thirsty for fame as a cricket is for cream; but, if it comes to a fair question, whether you are to please the mob, or do the thing as you know it ought to be done; and you can't do both, and choose to please the mob—it's all over with you;—there's no hope for you; nothing that you can do will ever be worth a man's glance as he passes by. The test is absolute, inevitable—Is your art first with you? Then you are artists; you may be, after you have made your money, misers and usurers; you may be, after you have got your fame, jealous, and proud, and wretched, and base: but yet, *as long as you won't spoil your work*, you are artists. On the other hand—Is your money first with you, and your fame first with you? Then, you may be very charitable with your money, and very magnificent with your money, and very graceful in the way you wear your reputation, and very courteous to those beneath you, and very acceptable to those above you; but you are *not artists*. You are mechanics, and drudges.

You must love the creation you work in the midst of. For wholly in proportion to the intensity of feeling which you bring to the subject you have chosen, will be the depth and justice of your perception of its character. And this depth of feeling is not to be gained on the instant, when you want to bring it to bear on this or that. It is the result of the general habit of striving to feel rightly; and, among thousands of various means of doing this, perhaps the one I ought specially to name to you, is the keeping yourselves clear of petty and mean cares. Whatever you do, don't be anxious, nor fill your heads with little chagrins and little desires. I have just said, that you may be great artists, and yet be miserly and jealous, and troubled about many things. So you may be; but I said also that the miserliness or trouble must not be in your hearts all day. It is possible that you may get a habit of saving money; or it is possible, at a time of great trial, you may yield to the temptation of speaking unjustly of a rival—and you will shorten your powers and dim your sight even by this; but the thing that you have to dread far more than any such uncon-scious habit, or any such momentary fall—is the *constancy of small emotions*; the anxiety whether Mr. So-and-so will like your work; whether such and such a workman will do all that you want of him; and so on; not wrong feelings or anxieties in themselves, but impertinent, and wholly incompatible with the full exercise of your imagination.

Keep yourselves, therefore, quiet, peaceful, with your eyes open. It doesn't matter at all what Mr. So-and-so thinks of your work; but it matters a great deal what that bird is doing up there in its nest, or how that vagabond child at the street corner is managing his game of knuckle-down. And remember, you cannot turn aside from your own interests, to the birds' and the children's interests, unless you have long before got into the habit of loving and watching birds and children; so that it all comes at last to the forgetting yourselves, and the living out of yourselves, in the calm of the great world, or if you will, in its agitation; but always in a calm of your own bringing. Do not think it wasted time to submit yourselves to any influence which may bring upon you any noble feeling. Rise early, always watch the sunrise, and the way the clouds break from the dawn; you will cast your statue-draperies in quite another than your common way, when the remembrance of that cloud motion is with you, and of the scarlet vesture of the morning. Live always in the springtime in the country; you do not know what leaf-form means, unless you have seen the buds burst, and the young leaves breathing low in the sunshine, and wondering at the first shower of rain. But above all, accustom yourselves to look for, and to love, all nobleness of gesture and feature in the human form; and remember that the highest nobleness is usually among the aged, the poor, and the infirm; you will find, in the end, that it is not the strong arm of the soldier, nor the laugh of the young beauty, that are the best studies for you. Look at them, and look at them reverently; but be assured that endurance is nobler than strength and patience than beauty; and that it is not in the high church pews, where the gay dresses are, but in the church free seats, where the widows' weeds are, that you may see the faces that will fit best between the angels' wings, in the church porch.

And therefore, lastly and chiefly, you must love the creatures to whom you minister, your fellow-men; for, if you do not love them, not only will you be little interested in the passing events of life, but in all your gazing at humanity, you will be apt to be struck only by outside form, and not by expression. It is only kindness and tenderness which will ever enable you to see what beauty there is in the dark eyes that are sunk with weeping, and in the paleness of those fixed faces which the earth's adversity has compassed about, till they shine in their patience like dying watchfires through twilight. But it is not this only which makes it needful for you, if you would be great, to be also kind; there is a most important and all-essential reason in the very nature of your own art. So soon as you desire to build largely, and with addition of noble sculpture, you will find that your work must be associative. You cannot carve a whole cathedral yourself—you can carve but few and simple parts of it. Either your own work must be disgraced in the mass of the collateral inferiority, or you must raise your fellow-designers to correspondence of power. If you have genius, you will yourselves take the lead in the building you design; you will carve its porch and direct its disposition. But for all subsequent advancement of its detail, you must trust to the agency and the invention of others; and it rests with you either to repress what faculties your workmen have, into cunning subordination to your own; or to rejoice in discovering even the powers that may rival you, and leading forth mind after mind into fellowship with your fancy, and association with your fame.

I need not tell you that if you do the first—if you endeavour to depress or disguise the talents of your subordinates—you are lost; for nothing could imply more darkly and decisively than this, that your art and your work were not beloved by you; that it was your own prosperity that you were seeking, and your own skill only that you cared to contemplate. I do not say that you must not be jealous at all: it is rarely in human nature to be wholly without jealousy; and you may be forgiven for going some day sadly home, when you find some youth, unpractised and unapproved, giving the life-stroke to his work which you, after years of training, perhaps, cannot reach: but your jealousy must not conquer—your love of your building must conquer, helped by your kindness of heart. See —I set no high or difficult standard before you. I do not say that you are to surrender your pre-eminence in *mere* unselfish generosity. But I do say that you must surrender your pre-eminence in your love of your building, helped by your kindness; and that whomsoever you find better able to do what will adorn it than you—that person you are to give place to: and to console yourselves for the humiliation, first, by your joy in seeing the edifice growing more beautiful under his chisel; and secondly, by your sense of having done kindly and justly.

But if you are morally strong enough to make the kindness and justice the first motive, it will be better—best of all—if you do not consider it as kindness at all, but bare and stern justice; for, truly, such help as we can give each other in this world is a *debt* to each other; and the man who perceives a superiority or capacity in a subordinate, and neither confesses nor assists it, is not merely the withholder of kindness, but the committer of injury. But be the motive what you will, only see that you do the thing; and take the joy of the consciousness that, as your art embraces a wider field than all others—and addresses a vaster multitude than all others—and is surer of audience than all others—so it is profounder and holier in Fellowship than all others. The artist, when his pupil is perfect, must see him leave his side that he may declare his distinct, perhaps opponent skill. Man of science wrestles with man of science for priority of discovery, and pursues in pangs of jealous haste his solitary inquiry. You alone are called by kindness—by necessity—by equity, to fraternity of toil; and thus, in those misty and massive piles which rise above the domestic roofs of our ancient cities, there was—there may be again—a meaning more profound and true than any that fancy so commonly has attached to them. Men say their pinnacles point to heaven. Why, so does every tree that buds, and every bird that rises as it sings. Men say their aisles are good for worship. Why, so is every mountain glen, and rough sea-shore. But this they have, of distinct and indisputable glory—that their mighty walls were never raised and never shall be, but by men who love and aid each other in their weakness;—that all their interlacing strength of vaulted stone has its foundation upon the stronger arches of manly fellowship, and all their changing grace of depressed or lifted pinnacle owes its cadence and completeness to sweeter symmetries of human soul.

From *Unto This Last.* 1860

THE ROOTS OF HONOUR

AMONG THE DELUSIONS WHICH AT DIFFERENT PERIODS have possessed themselves of the minds of large masses of the human race, perhaps the most curious—certainly the least creditable—is the modern *soi-disant* science of political economy, based on the idea that an advantageous code of social action may be determined irrespectively of the influence of social affection.

Of course, as in the instances of alchemy, astrology, witchcraft, and other such popular creeds, political economy has a plausible idea at the root of it. 'The social affections,' says the economist, 'are accidental and disturbing elements in human nature; but avarice and the desire of progress are constant elements. Let us eliminate the inconstants, and, considering the human being merely as a covetous machine, examine by what laws of labour, purchase, and sale, the greatest accumulative result in wealth is obtainable. Those laws once determined, it will be for each individual afterwards to introduce as much of the disturbing affectionate element as he chooses, and to determine for himself the result on the new conditions supposed.'

This would be a perfectly logical and successful method of analysis, if the accidentals afterwards to be introduced were of the same nature as the powers first examined. Supposing a body in motion to be influenced by constant and inconstant forces, it is usually the simplest way of examining its course to trace it first under the persistent conditions, and afterwards introduce the causes of variation. But the disturbing elements in the social

F   65

problem are not of the same nature as the constant ones: they alter the essence of the creature under examination the moment they are added; they operate, not mathematically, but chemically, introducing conditions which render all our previous knowledge unavailable. We made learned experiments upon pure nitrogen, and have convinced ourselves that it is a very manageable gas: but, behold! the thing which we have practically to deal with is its chloride; and this, the moment we touch it on our established principles, sends us and our apparatus through the ceiling.

Observe, I neither impugn nor doubt the conclusion of the science if its terms are accepted. I am simply uninterested in them, as I should be in those of a science of gymnastics which assumed that men had no skeletons. It might be shown, on that supposition, that it would be advantageous to roll the students up into pellets, flatten them into cakes, or stretch them into cables; and that when these results were effected, the re-insertion of the skeleton would be attended with various inconveniences to their constitution. The reasoning might be admirable, the conclusions true, and the science deficient only in applicability. Modern political economy stands on a precisely similar basis. Assuming, not that the human being has no skeleton, but that it is all skeleton, it founds an ossifiant theory of progress on this negation of a soul; and having shown the utmost that may be made of bones, and constructed a number of interesting geometrical figures with death's-head and humeri, successfully proves the inconvenience of the re-appearance of a soul among these corpuscular structures. I do not deny the truth of this theory: I simply deny its applicability to the present phase of the world.]

This inapplicability has been curiously manifested during the embarrassment caused by the late strikes of our workmen. Here occurs one of the simplest cases, in a pertinent and positive form, of the first vital problem which political economy has to deal with (the relation between employer and employed); and, at a severe crisis, when lives in multitudes and wealth in masses are at stake, the political economists are helpless—practically mute: no demonstrable solution of the difficulty can be given by them, such as may convince or calm the opposing parties. Obstinately the masters take one view of the matter; obstinately the operatives another; and no political science can set them at one.

It would be strange if it could, it being not by 'science' of any kind that men were ever intended to be set at one. Disputant after disputant vainly strives to show that the interests of the masters are, or are not, antagonistic to those of the men: none of the pleaders ever seeming to remember that it does not absolutely or always follow that the persons must be antagonistic because their interests are. If there is only a crust of bread in the house, and mother and children are starving, their interests are not the same. If the mother eats it, the children want it; if the children eat it, the mother must go hungry to her work. Yet it does not necessarily follow that there will be 'antagonism' between them, that they will fight for the crust, and that the mother, being the strongest, will get it, and eat it. Neither, in any other case, whatever the relations of the persons may be, can it be assumed for certain that, because their interests are diverse, they must necessarily regard each other with hostility, and use violence or cunning to obtain the advantage.

Even if this were so, and it were as just as it is convenient to consider men as actuated by no other moral influences than those which affect rats or swine, the logical conditions of the question are still indeterminable. It can never be shown generally either that the interests of master and labourer are alike, or that they are opposed; for, according to circumstances, they may be either. It is, indeed, always the interest of both that the work should be rightly done, and a just price obtained for it; but, in the division of profits, the gain of one may or may not

67

be the loss of the other. It is not the master's interest to pay wages so low as to leave the men sickly and depressed, nor the workman's interest to be paid high wages if the smallness of the master's profit hinders him from enlarging his business, or conducting it in a sage and liberal way. A stoker ought not to desire high pay if the company is too poor to keep the engine-wheels in repair.

And the varieties of circumstance which influence these reciprocal interests are so endless, that all endeavour to deduce rules of action from balance of expediency is in vain. And it is meant to be in vain. For no human actions ever were intended by the Maker of men to be guided by balances of expediency, but by balances of justice. He has therefore rendered all endeavours to determine expediency futile for evermore. No man ever knew, or can know, what will be the ultimate result to himself, or to others, of any given line of conduct. But every man may know, and most of us do know, what is a just and unjust act. And all of us may know also, that the consequences of justice will be ultimately the best possible, both to others and ourselves, though we can neither say what *is* best, nor how it is likely to come to pass.

I have said balances of justice, meaning, in the term justice to include affection—such affection as one man *owes* to another. All right relations between master and operative, and all their best interests, ultimately depend on these.

We shall find the best and simplest illustration of the relations of master and operative in the position of domestic servants.

We will suppose that the master of a household desires only to get as much work out of his servants as he can, at the rate of wages he gives. He never allows them to be idle; feeds them as poorly and lodges them as ill as they will endure; and in all things pushes his requirements to the exact point beyond which he cannot go without forcing the servant to leave him. In doing this, there is no violation on his part of what is commonly called 'justice'. He agrees with the domestic for his whole time and service, and takes them—the limits of hardship in treatment being fixed by the practice of other masters in his neighbourhood; that is to say, by the current rate of wages for domestic labour. If the servant can get a better place, he is free to take one, and the master can only tell what is the real market value of his labour, by requiring as much as he will give.

This is the politico-economical view of the case, according to the doctors of that science; who assert by this procedure the greatest average of work will be obtained from the servant and therefore the greatest benefit to the community and through the community, by reversion, to the servant himself.

That, however, is not so. It would be so if the servant were an engine of which the motive power was steam, magnetism, gravitation, or any other agent of calculable force. But he being, on the contrary, an engine whose motive power is a Soul, the force of this very peculiar agent, as an unknown quantity, enters into all the political economists' equations without his knowledge, and falsifies every one of their results. The largest quantity of work will not be done by this curious engine for pay, or under pressure, or by help of any kind of fuel which may be supplied by the chaldron. It will be done only when the motive force, that is to say, the will or spirit of creature, is brought to its greatest strength by its own proper fuel: namely, by the affections.

It may indeed happen, and does happen often, that if the master is a man of sense and energy, a large quantity of material work may be done under mechanical pressure, enforced by strong will and guided by wise method; also it may happen, and does happen often, that if the master is indolent and weak (however good-natured), a very small quantity of work and that bad, may be produced by the servant's undirected strength, and contemptuous gratitude. But the universal law of the matter is that, assuming any given quantity of energy and sense in master and servant, the greatest material result obtainable by them will be, not through antagonism to each other, but through affection for each other; and that, if the master, instead of endeavouring to get as much work as possible from the servant, seeks rather to render his appointed and necessary work beneficial to him, and to forward his interests in all just and wholesome ways, the real amount of work ultimately done, or of good rendered, by the person so cared for, will indeed be the greatest possible.

Observe, I say, 'of good rendered', for a servant's work is not necessarily or always the best thing he can give his master. But good of all kinds, whether in material service, in protective watchfulness of his master's interest and credit, or in joyful readiness to seize unexpected and irregular occasions of help.

Nor is this one whit less generally true because indulgence will be frequently abused, and kindness met with ingratitude. For the servant, who gently treated, is ungrateful, treated ungently, will be revengeful; and the man who is dishonest to a liberal master will be injurious to an unjust one.

In any case, and with any person, this unselfish treatment will produce the most effective return. Observe, I am here considering the affections wholly as a motive power; not at all as things in themselves desirable or noble, or in any other way abstractedly good. I look at them simply as an anomalous force, rendering every one of the ordinary political economist's calculations nugatory; while, even if he desired to introduce this new element into his estimates, he has no power of dealing with it; for the affections only become a true motive power when they ignore every other motive and condition of political economy. Treat the servant kindly, with the idea of turning his gratitude to account, and you will get, as you deserve, no gratitude, nor any value for your kindness; but treat him kindly without any economical purpose, and all economical purposes will be answered; in this, as in all other matters, whosoever will save his life shall lose it, who so loses it shall find it.

The next clearest and simplest example of relation between master and operative is that which exists between the commander of a regiment and his men.

Supposing the officer only desires to play the rules of discipline so as, with least trouble to himself, to make the regiment most effective, he will not be able, by any rules or administration of rules, on this selfish principle, to develop the full strength of his subordinates. If a man of sense and firmness, he may, as in the former instance, produce a better result than would be obtained by the irregular kindness of a weak officer; but let the sense and firmness be the same in both cases, and assuredly the officer who has the most direct personal relations with his men, the most care for their interests, and the most value for their lives, will develop their effective strength, through their affection for his own person, and trust in his character, to a degree wholly unattainable by other means. This law applies still more stringently as the numbers concerned are larger: a charge may often be successful, though the men dislike their officers; a battle has rarely been won, unless they loved their general.

Passing from these simple examples to the more complicated relations existing between a manufacturer and his workmen, we are met first by certain curious difficulties, resulting, apparently, from a harder and colder state of moral elements. It is easy to imagine an enthusiastic affection existing among soldiers for the colonel. Not so easy to imagine an enthusiastic affection among cotton-spinners for the proprietor of the mill. A body of men associated for purposes of robbery (as a Highland clan in ancient times) shall be animated by perfect affection, and every member of it be ready to lay down his life for the life of his chief. But a band of men associated for purposes of legal production and accumulation is usually animated, it appears, by no such emotions, and none of them are in any wise willing to give his life for the life of his chief. Not only are we met by this apparent anomaly, in moral matters, but by others connected with it, in administration of system. For a servant or a soldier is engaged at a definite rate of wages, for a definite period; but a workman at a rate of wages variable according to the demand for labour, and with the risk of being at any time thrown out of his situation by chances of trade. Now, as under these contingencies, no action of the affections can take place, but only an explosive action of *dis*affections, two points offer themselves for consideration in the matter.

The first—How far the rate of wages may be so regulated as not to vary with the demand for labour.

The second—How far it is possible that bodies of workmen may be engaged and maintained at such fixed rates of wages (whatever the state of trade may be), without enlarging or diminishing their number, so as to give them permanent interest in the establishment with which they are connected, like that of the domestic servants in an old family, or an *esprit de corps*, like that of the soldiers in a crack regiment.

The first question is, I say, how far it may be possible to fix the rate of wages, irrespectively of the demand for labour.

Perhaps one of the most curious facts in the history of human error is the denial by the common political economist of the possibility of thus regulating wages; while, for all the important, and much of the unimportant, labour, on the earth, wages are already so regulated.

We do not sell our prime-ministership by Dutch auction; nor, on the decease of a bishop, whatever may be the general advantages of simony, do we (yet) offer his diocese to the clergyman who will take the episcopacy at the lowest contract. We (with exquisite sagacity of political economy!) do indeed sell commissions; but not openly, generalships: sick, we do not inquire for a physician who takes less than a guinea; litigious, we never think of reducing six-and-eight-pence to four-and-sixpence; caught in a shower, we do not canvass the cabmen, to find one who values his driving at less than sixpence a mile.

It is true that in all these cases there is, and in every conceivable case there must be, ultimate reference to the presumed difficulty of the work, or number of candidates for the office. If it were thought that the labour necessary to make a good physician would be gone through by a sufficient number of students with the prospect of only half-guinea fees, public consent would soon withdraw the unnecessary half-guinea. In this ultimate sense, the price of labour is indeed always regulated by the demand for it; but, so far as the practical and immediate administration of the matter is regarded, the best labour always has been, and is, as *all* labour ought to be, paid by an invariable standard.

'What!' the reader perhaps answers amazedly: 'pay good and bad workmen alike?'

Certainly. The difference between one prelate's sermons and his successor's—or between one physician's opinion and another's—is far greater, as respects the qualities of mind involved, and far more important in result to you personally, than the difference between good and bad laying of bricks (though that is greater than most people suppose). Yet you pay with equal fee, contentedly, the good and bad workmen upon your soul, and the good and bad workmen upon your body; much more may you pay, contentedly, with equal fees, the good and bad workmen upon your house.

'Nay, but I choose my physician, and (?) my clergyman, thus indicating my sense of the quality of their work.' By all means, also, choose your bricklayer: that is the proper reward of the good workman, to be 'chosen'. The natural and right system respecting all labour is, that it should be paid at a fixed rate, but the good workman employed, and the bad workman unemployed. The false, unnatural, and destructive system is when the bad workman is allowed to offer his work at half-price, and either take the place of the good, or force him by his competition to work for an inadequate sum.

This equality of wages, then, being the first object towards which we have to discover the directest available road, the second is, as above stated, that of maintaining constant numbers of workmen in employment, whatever may be the accidental demand for the article they produce.

I believe the sudden and extensive inequalities of demand, which necessarily arise in the mercantile operations of an active nation, constitute the only essential difficulty which has to be overcome in a just organization of labour.

The subject opens into too many branches to admit of being investigated in a paper of this kind; but the following general facts bearing on it may be noted.

The wages which enable any workman to live are necessarily higher, if his work is liable to intermission, than if it is assured and continuous; and however severe the struggle for work may become, the general law will always hold, that men must get more daily pay if, on the average, they can only calculate on work three days a week than they would require if they were sure of work six days a week. Supposing that a man cannot live on less than a shilling a day, his seven shillings he must get, either for three days' violent work, or six days' deliberate work. The tendency of all modern mercantile operations is to throw both wages and trade into the form of a lottery, and to make the workman's pay depend on intermittent exertion, and the principal's profit on dexterously used chance.

In what partial degree, I repeat, this may be necessary in

consequence of the activities of modern trade, I do not here investigate; contenting myself with the fact that in its fatallest aspects it is assuredly unnecessary, and results merely from love of gambling on the part of the masters, and from ignorance and sensuality in the men. The masters cannot bear to let any opportunity of gain escape them, and frantically rush at every gap and breach in the walls of Fortune, raging to be rich, and affronting, with impatient covetousness, every risk of ruin, while the men prefer three days of violent labour, and three days of drunkenness, to six days of moderate work and wise rest. There is no way in which a principal, who really desires to help his workmen, may do it more effectually than by checking these disorderly habits both in himself and them; keeping his own business operations on a scale which will enable him to pursue them securely, not yielding to temptations of precarious gain; and at the same time, leading his workmen into regular habits of labour and life, either by inducing them rather to take low wages, in the form of a fixed salary, than high wages, subject to the chance of their being thrown out of work; or, if this be impossible, by discouraging the system of violent exertion for nominally high day wages, and leading the men to take lower pay for more regular labour.

In effecting any radical changes of this kind, doubtless there would be great inconvenience and loss incurred by all the originators of the movement. That which can be done with perfect convenience and without loss, is not always the thing that most needs to be done, or which we are most imperatively required to do.

I have already alluded to the difference hitherto existing between regiments of men associated for purposes of violence, and for purposes of manufacture; in that the former appear capable of self-sacrifice—the latter, not; which singular fact is the real reason of the general lowness of estimate in which the profession of commerce is held, as compared with that of arms. Philosophically, it does not, at first sight, appear reasonable (many writers have endeavoured to prove it unreasonable) that a peaceable and rational person, whose trade is buying and selling, should be held in less honour than an unpeaceable and often irrational person, whose trade is slaying. Nevertheless, the consent of mankind has always, in spite of the philosophers, given precedence to the soldier.

And this is right.

For the soldier's trade, verily and essentially, is not slaying, but being slain. This, without well knowing its own meaning, the world honours it for. A bravo's trade is slaying; but the world has never respected bravos more than merchants: the reason it honours the soldier is, because he holds his life at the service of the State. Reckless he may be—fond of pleasure or of adventure—all kinds of by-motives and mean impulses may have determined the choice of his profession, and may affect (to all appearance exclusively) his daily conduct in it; but our estimate of him is based on this ultimate fact— of which we are well assured—that put him in a fortress breach, with all the pleasures of the world behind him, he will keep his face to the front; and he knows that his choice may be put to him at any moment—and has beforehand taken his part—virtually takes such part continually—does, in reality, die daily.

Not less is the respect we pay to the lawyer and physician, founded ultimately on their self-sacrifice. Whatever the learning or acuteness of a great lawyer, our chief respect for him depends on our belief that, set in a judge's seat, he will strive to judge justly, come of it what may. Could we suppose that he would take bribes, and use his acuteness and legal knowledge to give plausibility to iniquitous decisions, no degree of intellect would win for him our respect. Nothing will win it, short of our tacit conviction, that in all important acts of his life justice is first with him; his own interest second.

In the case of a physician, the ground of the honour we render him is clearer still. Whatever his science, we would shrink from him in horror if we found him regard his patients merely as subjects to experiment upon; much more, if we found that, receiving bribes from persons interested in their deaths, he was using his best skill to give poison in the mask of medicine.

Finally, the principle holds with utmost clearness as it respects clergymen. No goodness of disposition will excuse want of science in a physician, or of shrewdness in an advocate; but a clergyman, even though his power of intellect be small, is respected on the presumed ground of his unselfishness and serviceableness.

Now there can be no question but that the tact, foresight, decision, and other mental powers, required for the successful management of a large mercantile concern, if not such as could be compared with those of a great lawyer, general, or divine, would at least match the general conditions of mind required in the subordinate officers of a ship, or of a regiment, or in the curate of a country parish. If, therefore, all the efficient members of the so-called liberal professions are still, somehow, in public estimate of honour, preferred before the head of a commercial firm, the reason must lie deeper than in the measurement of their several powers of mind.

And the essential reason for such preference will be found to lie in the fact that the merchant is presumed to act always selfishly. His work may be very necessary to the community; but the motive of it is understood to be wholly personal. The merchant's first object in all his dealings must be (the public believe) to get as much for himself, and leave as little to his neighbour (or customer) as possible. Enforcing this upon him, by political statute, as the necessary principle of his action; recommending it to him on all occasions, and themselves reciprocally adopting it, proclaiming vociferously, for law of the universe, that a buyer's function is to cheapen, and a seller's to cheat—the public, nevertheless, involuntarily condemn the man of commerce for his compliance with their own statement, and stamp him for ever as belonging to an inferior grade of human personality.

This they will find, eventually, they must give up doing. They must not cease to condemn selfishness; but they will have to discover a kind of commerce which is not exclusively selfish. Or, rather, they will have to discover that there never was, or can be, any other kind of commerce; that this which they have called commerce was not commerce at all, but cozening; and that a true merchant differs as much from a merchant according to laws of modern political economy, as the hero of the 'Excursion' from Autolycus. They will find that commerce is an occupation which gentlemen will every day see more need to engage in, rather than in the businesses of talking to men, or slaying them; that, in true commerce, as in true preaching, or true fighting, it is necessary to admit the idea of occasional voluntary loss; that sixpences have to be lost, as well as lives, under a sense of duty; that the market may have its martyrdoms as well as the pulpit; and trade its heroisms as well as war.

May have—in the final issue, must have—and only has not had yet, because men of heroic temper have always been misguided in their youth into other fields; not recognizing what is in our days, perhaps, the most important of all fields; so that, while many a zealous person loses his life in trying to teach the form of a gospel, very few will lose a hundred pounds in showing the practice of one.

The fact is, that people never have had clearly explained to them the true functions of a merchant with respect to other people. I should like the reader to be very clear about this.

Five great intellectual professions, relating to daily necessities of life, have hitherto existed—three exist necessarily, in every civilized nation.

The Soldier's profession is to *defend* it.

The Pastor's to *teach* it.

The Physician's to *keep it in health*.

The Lawyer's to *enforce justice in it*.

The Merchant's to *provide* for it.

And the duty of all these men is, on due occasion, to *die* for it.

'On due occasion,' namely:—

The Soldier, rather than leave his post in battle.

The Physician, rather than leave his post in plague.

The Pastor, rather than teach Falsehood.

The Lawyer, rather than countenance Injustice.

The Merchant—what is *his* 'due occasion' of death?

It is the main question for the merchant, as for all of us. For, truly, the man who does not know when to die, does not know how to live.

Observe, the merchant's function (or manufacturer's, for in the broad sense in which it is here used the word must be understood to include both) is to provide for the nation. It is no more his function to get profit for himself out of that provision than it is a clergyman's function to get his stipend. This stipend is a due and necessary adjunct, but not the object of his life, if he be a true clergyman, any more than his fee (or honorarium) is the object of life to a true physician. Neither is his fee the object of life to a true merchant. All three, if true men, have a work to be done irrespective of fee—to be done even at any cost, or for quite the contrary of fee; the pastor's function being to teach, the physician's to heal, and the merchant's, as I have said, to provide. That is to say, he has to understand to their very root the qualities of the thing he deals in, and the means of obtaining or producing it; and he has to apply all his sagacity and energy to the producing or obtaining

79

it in perfect state, and distributing it at the cheapest possible price where it is most needed.

And because the production or obtaining of any commodity involves necessarily the agency of many lives and hands, the merchant becomes in the course of his business the master and governor of large masses of men in a more direct, though less confessed way, than a military officer or pastor; so that on him falls, in great part, the responsibility for the kind of life they lead; and it becomes his duty, not only to be always considering how to produce what he sells, in the purest and cheapest forms, but how to make the various employments involved in the production, or transference of it, most beneficial to the men employed.

And as into these two functions, requiring for their right exercise the highest intelligence, as well as patience, kindness and tact, the merchant is bound to put all his energy, so for their just discharge he is bound, as soldier or physician is bound, to give up, if need be, his life, in such way as it may be demanded of him. Two main points he has in his providing function to maintain: first, his engagements (faithfulness to engagements being the real root of all possibilities, in commerce); and, secondly, the perfectness and purity of the thing provided; so that, rather than fail in any engagement, or consent to any deterioration, adulteration, or unjust and exorbitant price of that which he provides, he is bound to meet fearlessly any form of distress, poverty, or labour, which may, through maintenance of these points, come upon him.

Again: in his office as governor of the men employed by him, the merchant or manufacturer is invested with a distinctly paternal authority and responsibility. In most cases, a youth entering a commercial establishment is withdrawn altogether from home influence; his master must become his father, else he has, for practical and constant help, no father at hand: in all cases the master's authority, together with the eneral tone and atmosphere of his business, and the character f the men with whom the youth is compelled in the course f it to associate, have more immediate and pressing weight an the home influence, and will usually neutralize it either or good or evil; so that the only means which the master has f doing justice to the men employed by him is to ask himself ernly whether he is dealing with such subordinate as he ould with his own son, if compelled by circumstances to ke such a position.

Supposing the captain of a frigate saw it right, or were by ny chance obliged, to place his own son in the position of common sailor: as he would then treat his son, he is bound lways to treat every one of the men under him. So, also, sup- osing the master of a manufactory saw it right, or were by ny chance obliged, to place his own son in the position of an rdinary workman; as he would then treat his son, he is bound lways to treat every one of his men. This is the only effective, ue, or practical RULE which can be given on this point of olitical economy.

And as the captain of a ship is bound to be the last man to ave his ship in case of wreck, and to share his last crust with he sailors in case of famine, so the manufacturer, in any ommercial crisis or distress, is bound to take the suffering of with his men, and even to take more of it for himself than e allows his men to feel; as a father would in a famine, or attle, sacrifice himself for his son.

All which sounds very strange: the only real strangeness a the matter being, nevertheless, that it should so sound. For ll that is true, and that not partially nor theoretically, but verlastingly and practically: all other doctrine than this especting matters political being false in premises, absurd in eduction, and impossible in practice, consistently with any rogressive state of national life; all the life which we now ossess as a nation showing itself in the resolute denial and

scorn, by a few strong minds and faithful hearts, of the economic principles taught to our multitudes, which principles, so
far as accepted, lead straight to national destruction. Respecting
the modes and forms of destruction to which they lead, and
on the other hand, respecting the further practical working
of true polity, I hope to reason further in a following paper.

From *The Queen of the Air*. 1869

ATHENA KERAMITIS

NOW WE HAVE TWO ORDERS OF ANIMALS TO TAKE SOME
note of in connection with Athena, and one vast order of
plants, which will illustrate this matter very sufficiently for us.

The two orders of animals are the serpent and the bird; the
serpent, in which the breath or spirit is less than in any other
creature, and the earth-power greatest:—the bird, in which
the breath, or spirit, is more full than in any other creature, and
the earth-power least.

We will take the bird first. It is little more than a drift of the
air brought into form by plumes; the air is in all its quills, it
breathes through its whole frame and flesh, and glows with
air in its flying, like a blown flame: it rests upon the air, sub-
dues it, surpasses it, outraces it: *is* the air, conscious of itself,
conquering itself, ruling itself.

Also, into the throat of the bird is given the voice of the
air. All that in the wind itself is weak, wild, useless in sweetness, is knit together in its song. As we may imagine the wild
form of the cloud closed into the perfect form of the bird's
wings, so the wild voice of the cloud into its ordered and commanded voice; unwearied, rippling through the clear heaven
in its gladness, interpreting all intense passion through the
soft spring nights, bursting into acclaim and rapture of choir
at daybreak, or lisping and twittering among the boughs and
hedges through heat of day, like little winds that only make the
cowslip bells shake, and ruffle the petals of the wild rose.

Also, upon the plumes of the bird are put the colours of the
air: on these the gold of the cloud, that cannot be gathered by
any covetousness; the rubies of the clouds, that are not the

83

price of Athena, but *are* Athena; the vermilion of the cloud-bar, and the flame of the cloud-crest, and the snow of the cloud, and its shadow, and the melted blue of the deep wells of the sky—all these, seized by the creating spirit, and woven by Athena herself into films and threads of plume; with wave on wave following and fading along breast, and throat, and opened wings, infinite as the dividing of the foam and the sifting of the sea-sand; even the white down of the cloud seeming to flutter up between the stronger plumes, seen, but too soft for touch.

And so the Spirit of the Air is put into, and upon, this created form; and it becomes, through twenty centuries, the symbol of divine help, descending, as the Fire, to speak, but as the Dove, to bless.

Next, in the serpent, we approach the source of a group of myths, world-wide, founded on great and common human instincts, respecting which I must note one or two points which bear intimately on all our subject. For it seems to me that the scholars who are at present occupied in interpretation of human myths have most of them forgotten that there are any such things as natural myths; and that the dark sayings of men may be both difficult to read, and not always worth reading; but the dark sayings of Nature will probably become clearer for the looking into, and will very certainly be worth reading. And, indeed, all guidance to the right sense of the human and variable myths will probably depend on our first getting at the sense of the natural and invariable ones. The dead hieroglyph may have meant this or that—the living hieroglyph means always the same; but remember, it is just as much a hieroglyph as the other; nay, more—a 'Sacred or reserved sculpture', a thing with an inner language. The serpent crest of the king's crown, or of the god's, on the pillars of Egypt, is a mystery; but the serpent itself, gliding past the pillar's foot, is it less a mystery? Is there, indeed, no tongue, except the mute forked flash from its lips, in that running brook of horror on the ground?

Why that horror? We all feel it, yet how imaginative it is, how disproportioned to the real strength of the creature! There is more poison in an ill-kept drain—in a pool of dish-washings at a cottage door, than in the deadliest asp of Nile. Every back-yard which you look down into from the railway, as it carries you out by Vauxhall or Deptford, holds its coiled serpent: all the walls of those ghastly suburbs are enclosures of tank temples for serpent-worship; yet you feel no horror in looking down into them, as you would if you saw the livid scales, and lifted head. There is more venom, mortal, inevitable, in a single word, sometimes, or in the gliding entrance of a word-less thought, than ever *vanti Libia con sua rena*. But that horror is of the myth, not of the creature. There are myriads lower than this, and more loathsome, in the scale of being; the links between dead matter and animation drift everywhere unseen. But it is the strength of the base element that is so dreadful in the serpent; it is the very omnipotence of the earth. That rivulet of smooth silver—how does it flow, think you? It literally rows on the earth, with every scale for an oar; it bites the dust with the ridges of its body. Watch it, when it moves slowly: A wave, but without wind! a current, but with no fall! all the body moving at the same instant, yet some of it to one side, some to another, or some forward, and the rest of the coil backwards; but all with the same calm will and equal way—no contraction, no extension; one soundless, causeless, march of sequent rings, and spectral procession of spotted dust, with dissolution in its fangs, dislocation in its coils. Startle it; the winding stream will become a twisted arrow; the wave of poisoned life will lash through the grass like a cast lance. It scarcely breathes with its one lung (the other shrivelled and abortive); it is passive to the sun and shade, and is cold or hot like a stone; yet 'it can outclimb the monkey, outswim the fish, outleap the zebra, outwrestle the athlete, and crush the tiger'. It is a divine hieroglyph of the demoniac power of the earth—of the entire earthly Nature. As the bird is the clothed power of the air, so this is the clothed power of the dust; as the bird the symbol of the spirit of life, so this of the grasp and sting of death.

Hence the continual change in the interpretation put upon it in various religions. As the worm of corruption, it is the mightiest of all adversaries of the gods—the special adversary of their light and creative power—Python against Apollo. As the power of the earth against the air, the giants are serpent-bodied in the *Giganto-machia*; but as the power of the earth upon the seed—consuming it into new life ('that which thou sowest is not quickened except it die')—serpents sustain the chariot of the spirit of agriculture.

Yet, on the other hand, there is a power in the earth to take away corruption, and to purify (hence the very fact of burial, and many uses of earth, only lately known); and in this sense, the serpent is a healing spirit—the representative of Æsculapius, and of Hygieia; and is a sacred earth-type in the temple of the Dew; being there especially a symbol of the native earth of Athens; so that its departure from the temple was a sign to the Athenians that they were to leave their homes. And then, lastly, as there is a strength and healing in the earth, no less than the strength of air, so there is conceived to be a wisdom of earth no less than a wisdom of the spirit; and when its deadly power is killed, its guiding power becomes true; so that the Python serpent is killed at Delphi, where yet the oracle is from the breath of the earth.

You must remember, however, that in this, as in every other instance, I take the myth at its central time. This is only the meaning of the serpent to the Greek mind which could conceive an Athena. Its first meaning to the nascent eyes of men, and its continued influence over degraded races, are subjects of the most fearful mystery. Mr. Fergusson has just collected the principal evidence bearing on the matter in a work of very great value, and if you read his opening chapters, they will put you in possession of the circumstances needing chiefly to be considered. I cannot touch upon any of them here, except only to point out that, though the doctrine of the so-called 'corruption of human nature', asserting that there is nothing but evil in humanity, is just as blasphemous and false as a doctrine of the corruption of physical nature would be, asserting there was nothing but evil in the earth—there is yet the clearest evidence of a disease, plague, or cretinous imperfection of development, hitherto allowed to prevail against the greater part of the races of men; and this in monstrous ways, more full of mystery than the serpent-being itself. I have gathered for you to-night only instances of what is beautiful in Greek religion; but even in its best time there were deep corruptions in other phases of it, and degraded forms of many of its deities, all originating in a misunderstood worship of the principle of life; while in the religions of lower races, little else than these corrupted forms of devotion can be found; all having a strange and dreadful consistency with each other, and infecting Christianity, even at its strongest periods, with fatal terror of doctrine, and ghastliness of symbolic conception, passing through fear into frenzied grotesque, and thence into sensuality.

In the Psalter of St. Louis itself, half of its letters are twisted snakes; there is scarcely a wreathed ornament, employed in Christian dress, or architecture, which cannot be traced back to the serpent's coil; and there is rarely a piece of monkish decorated writing in the world, that is not tainted with some ill-meant vileness of grotesque—nay, the very leaves of the twisted ivy-pattern of the fourteenth century can be followed back to wreaths for the foreheads of bacchanalian gods. And truly, it seems to me, as I gather in my mind the evidences of insane religion, degraded art, merciless war, sullen toil, detestable pleasure, and vain or vile hope, in which the nations of the world have lived since first they could bear record of themselves—it seems to me, I say, as if the race itself were still half-serpent, not extricated yet from its clay; a lacertine breed of bitterness—the glory of it emaciate with cruel hunger, and blotted with venomous stain: and the track of it, on the leaf a glittering slime, and in the sand a useless furrow.

From *Fors Clavigera*. 1871–1884

LETTER 20
[THE VISION OF ST. URSULA]

5th July [1872]

YESTERDAY, IN THESE BROKEN SENTENCES, I TRIED TO make you understand that for all human creatures there are necessarily three separate states: life positive, under blessing—life negative, under curse—and death, neutral between these; and, henceforward, take due note of the quite true assumption you make in your ordinary malediction, that the state of condemnation may begin in this world, and separately affect every living member of the body.

You assume the fact of these two opposite states, then; but you have no idea whatever of the meaning of your words, nor of the nature of the blessedness or condemnation you admit. I will try to make your conception clearer.

In the year 1869, just before leaving Venice, I had been carefully looking at a picture by Victor Carpaccio, representing the dream of a young princess. Carpaccio has taken much pains to explain to us, as far as he can, the kind of life she leads, by completely painting her little bedroom in the light of dawn, so that you can see everything in it. It is lighted by two doubly-arched windows, the arches being painted crimson round their edges, and the capitals of the shafts that bear them, gilded. They are filled at the top with small round panes of glass; but beneath, are open to the blue morning sky, with a low lattice across them: and in the one at the back of the room are set two beautiful white Greek vases with a plant in each; one having rich dark and pointed green leaves, the

89

other crimson flowers, but not of any species known to me, each at the end of a branch like a spray of heath.

These flower-pots stand on a shelf which runs all round the room, and beneath the window, at about the height of the elbow, and serves to put things on anywhere: beneath it; down to the floor, the walls are covered with green cloth, but above, are bare and white. The second window is nearly opposite the bed, and in front of it is the princess's reading-table, some two feet and a half square, covered by a red cloth with a white border and dainty fringe; and beside it her seat, not at all like a reading-chair in Oxford, but a very small three-legged stool like a music-stool, covered with crimson cloth. On the table are a book set up at a slope fittest for reading, and an hour-glass. Under the shelf, near the table, so as to be easily reached by the outstretched arm, is a press full of books. The door of this has been left open, and the books, I am grieved to say, are rather in disorder, having been pulled about before the princess went to bed, and one left standing on its side.

Opposite this window, on the white wall, is a small shrine or picture (I can't see which, for it is in sharp retiring perspective) with a lamp before it, and a silver vessel hung from the lamp, looking like one for holding incense.

The bed is a broad four-poster, the posts being beautifully wrought golden or gilded rods, variously wreathed and branched, carrying a canopy of warm red. The princess's shield is at the head of it, and the feet are raised entirely above the floor of the room, on a dais which projects at the lower end so as to form a seat, on which the child has laid her crown. Her little blue slippers lie at the side of the bed—her white dog beside them. The coverlid is scarlet, the white sheet folded half-way back over it; the young girl lies straight, bending neither at waist nor knee, the sheet rising and falling over her in a narrow unbroken wave, like the shape of the coverlid of the last sleep, when the turf scarcely rises. She is some seventeen or eighteen years old, her head is turned towards us on the pillow, the cheek resting on her hand, as if she were thinking, yet utterly calm in sleep, and almost colourless. Her hair is tied with a narrow riband, and divided into two wreaths, which encircle her head like a double crown. The white nightgown hides the arm raised on the pillow, down to the wrist.

At the door of the room an angel enters (the little dog, though lying awake, vigilant, takes no notice). He is a very small angel, his head just rises a little above the shelf round the room, and would only reach as high as the princess's chin, if she were standing up. He has soft grey wings, lustreless; and his dress, of subdued blue, has violet sleeves, open above the elbow, and showing white sleeves below. He comes in without haste, his body, like a mortal one, casting shadow from the light through the door behind, his face perfectly quiet; a palm-branch in his right hand—a scroll in his left.

So dreams the princess, with blessed eyes, that need no earthly dawn. It is very pretty of Carpaccio to make her dream out the angel's dress so particularly, and notice the slashed sleeves; and to dream so little an angel—very nearly a doll angel—bringing her the branch of palm, and message. But the lovely characteristic of all is the evident delight of her continual life. Royal power over herself, and happiness in her flowers, her books, her sleeping, and waking, her prayers, her dreams, her earth, her heaven.

After I had spent my morning over this picture, I had to go to Verona by the afternoon train. In the carriage with me were two American girls with their father and mother, people of the class which has lately made so much money, suddenly, and does not know what to do with it: and these two girls, of about fifteen and eighteen, had evidently been indulged in everything (since they had had the means) which Western civilization could imagine. And here they were, specimens of the utmost which the money and invention of the nineteenth century could produce in maidenhood—children of its most progressive race—enjoying the full advantages of political liberty, of enlightened philosophical education, of cheap pilfered literature, and of luxury at any cost. Whatever money, machinery, or freedom of thought could do for these two children, had been done. No superstition had deceived, no restraint degraded them: types, they could not but be, of maidenly wisdom and felicity, as conceived by the forwardest intellects of our time.

And they were travelling through a district which, if any in the world, should touch the hearts and delight the eyes of young girls. Between Venice and Verona! Portia's villas perhaps in sight upon the Brenta, Juliet's tomb to be visited in the evening—blue against the southern sky, the hills of Petrarch's home. Exquisite midsummer sunshine, with low rays, glanced through the vine-leaves; all the Alps were clear; from the Lake of Garda to Cadore, and to farthest Tyrol. What a princess's chamber, this, if these are princesses, and what dreams might they not dream, therein!

But the two American girls were neither princesses, nor seers, nor dreamers. By infinite self-indulgence, they had reduced themselves simply to two pieces of white putty that could feel pain. The flies and the dust stuck to them as to clay, and they perceived, between Venice and Verona, nothing but the flies and the dust. They pulled down the blinds the moment they entered the carriage, and then sprawled, and writhed, and tossed among the cushions of it, in vain contest, during the whole fifty miles, with every miserable sensation of bodily affliction that could make time intolerable. They were dressed in thin white frocks, coming vaguely open at the backs as they stretched or wriggled; they had French novels, lemons, and lumps of sugar, to beguile their state with; the novels hanging together by the ends of string that had once stitched them, or adhering at the corners in densely bruised dog's-ears, out of which the girls, wetting their fingers, occasionally extricated a gluey leaf. From time to time they cut a lemon open, ground a lump of sugar backwards and forwards over it till every fibre was in a treacly pulp; then sucked the pulp, and gnawed the white skin into leathery strings for the sake of its bitter. Only one sentence was exchanged, in the fifty miles, on the subject of things outside the carriage (the Alps being once visible from a station where they had drawn up the blinds).

'Don't those snow-caps make you cool?'

'No—I wish they did.'

And so they went their way, with sealed eyes and tormented limbs, their numbered miles of pain.

There are the two states for you, in clearest opposition; Blessed, and Accursed. The happy industry, and eyes full of sacred imagination of things that are not (such sweet *cosa è la fede*), and the tortured indolence, and infidel eyes, blind even to the things that are.

'How do I know the princess is industrious?'

Partly by the trim state of her room—by the hour-glass on the table—by the evident use of all the books she has (well bound, every one of them, in stoutest leather or velvet, and with no dog's ears), but more distinctly from another picture of her, not asleep. In that one, a prince of England has sent to ask her in marriage: and her father, little liking to part with her, sends for her to his room to ask her what she would do. He sits, moody and sorrowful; she, standing before him in a plain housewifely dress, talks quietly, going on with her needlework all the time.

A work-woman, friends, she, no less than a princess; and princess most in being so. In like manner, in a picture by a Florentine, whose mind I would fain have you know somewhat as well as Carpaccio's—Sandro Botticelli—the girl who is to be the wife of Moses, when he first sees her at the desert-well, has fruit in her left hand, but a distaff in her right.

'To do good work, whether you live or die', it is the entrance to all Princedoms; and if not done, the day will come, and that infallibly, when you must labour for evil instead of good.

It was some comfort to me, that second day of May last, at Pisa, to watch the workman's ashamed face, as he struck the old marble cross to pieces. Stolidly and languidly he dealt the blows—down-looking—so far as in anywise sensitive, ashamed —and well he might be.

It was a wonderful thing to see done. This Pisan chapel, first built in 1230, then called the Oracle, or Oratory—*Oraculum, vel Oratorium*—or the Blessed Mary of the New Bridge, afterwards called the Sea-bridge (*Pontr-a-Mare*), was a shrine like that of ours on the Bridge of Wakefield; a boatman's praying-place; you may still see, or might, ten years since, have seen, the use of such a thing at the mouth of Boulogne Harbour, when the mackerel boats went out in a fleet at early dawn. There used to be a little shrine at the end of the longest pier; and as the *Bonne-Espérance*, or *Grâce-de-Dieu* or *Vierge Marie*, or *Notre Dame des Dunes*, or *Reine des Anges*, rose on the first surge of the open sea, their crews bared their heads, and prayed for a few seconds. So also the Pisan oarsmen looked back to their shrine, many-pinnacled, standing out from the quay above the river, as they dropped down Arno under their sea-bridge, bound for the Isles of Greece. Later, in the fifteenth century, 'there was laid up in it a little branch of the Crown of Thorns of the Re- deemer, which a merchant had brought home, enclosed in a little urn of Beyond-sea' (ultramarine), and its name was changed to 'St. Mary's of the Thorn'.

In the year 1840 I first drew it, then as perfect as when it was built. Six hundred and ten years had only given the marble of it a tempered glow, or touched its sculpture here and there with softer shade. I daguerreotyped the eastern end of it some years later (photography being then unknown), and copied the daguerreotype, that people might not be plagued in looking, by the lustre. The frontispiece to this letter is engraved from the drawing, and will show you what the building was like.

But the last quarter of a century has brought changes, and made the Italians wiser. British Protestant missionaries explained to them that they had only got a piece of blackberry stem in their ultramarine box. German philosophical missionaries explained to them that the Crown of Thorns itself was only a graceful metaphor. French republican missionaries explained to them that chapels were inconsistent with liberty on the quay; and their own engineering missionaries of civilization explained to them that steam-power was independent of the Madonna. And now in 1872, rowing by steam, digging by steam, driving by steam, here, behold, are a troublesome pair of human arms out of employ. So the engineering missionaries fit them with hammer and chisel, and set them to break up the Spina Chapel.

A costly kind of stone-breaking, this, for Italian parishes to set paupers on! Are there not rocks enough of Apennine, think you, they could break down instead? For truly, the God of their Fathers, and of their land, would rather see them mar His own work, than His children's.

Believe me, faithfully yours,

JOHN RUSKIN.

From *Fors Clavigera*

LETTER 80 [THE NAIL-MAKERS]

Bellefield, Birmingham, 16th July, 1877

I NEVER YET SATE DOWN TO WRITE MY '*FORS*', OR INdeed to write anything, in so broken and puzzled a state of mind as that in which this morning, I have been for the last ten minutes idly listening to the plash of the rain; and watching the workmen on the new Gothic school, which is fast blocking out the one pretty country view from my window.

I have been staying for two days with the good Mayor of Birmingham: and he has shown me St. George's land, his gift, in the midst of a sweet space of English hill and dale and orchard, yet unhurt by hand of man: and he has brought a representative group of the best men of Birmingham to talk to me; and they have been very kind to me, and have taught me much: and I feel just as I can fancy a poor Frenchman of some gentleness and sagacity might have felt, in Nelson's time—taken prisoner by his mortal enemies, and beginning to apprehend that there was indeed some humanity in Englishmen, and some providential and inscrutable reason for their existence.

You may think it strange that a two days' visit should produce such an effect on me; and say (which indeed will be partly true) that I ought to have made this visit before now. But, all things considered, I believe it has been with exactness, timely: and you will please remember that just in proportion to the quantity of work and thought we have spent on any subject, is the quantity we can further learn about it in a little while, and the power with which new facts, or new light cast on those already known, will modify past conclusions. And

96

when these facts are wholly trustworthy, and the lights thrown precisely where one asks for them, a day's talk may sometimes do as much as a year's work.

The one great fact which I have been most clearly impressed by, here, is the right-mindedness of these men, so far as they see what they are doing. There is no equivocation with their consciences—no silencing of their thoughts in any wilful manner; nor, under the conditions apparent to them, do I believe it possible for them to act more wisely or faithfully. That some conditions, non-apparent to them, may give unexpectedly harmful consequences to their action, is wholly the fault of others.

Meantime, recovering myself as a good ship tries to do after she has been struck by a heavy sea, I must say to my Birmingham friends a few things which I could not, while I was bent on listening and hearing; could not, also, in courtesy, but after deliberation had: so that, in all our debate, I was under this disadvantage, that they could say to me, with full pleasure and frankness, all that was in their minds; but I could not say, without much fear and pause, what was in mine. Of which unspoken regrets this is the quite initial and final one; that all they showed me, and told me of good, involved yet the main British modern idea that the master and his men should belong to two entirely different classes; perhaps loyally related to and assisting each other; but yet—the one, on the whole, living in hardship of the other in ease; the one uncomfortable—the other in comfort; the one supported in its dishonourable condition by the hope of labouring through it to the higher one—the other honourably distinguished by their success, and rejoicing in their escape from a life which must nevertheless be always (as they suppose) led by a thousand to one[1] of the British people.

[1] I do not use this as a rhetorical expression: Take the lower shop-keepers with the operatives, and add the great army of the merely helpless and miserable; and I believe 'a thousand to one' of the disgraced and

Whereas St. George, whether in agriculture, architecture, or manufacture, concerns himself only with the life of the work-man—refers all to that—measures all by that—holds the Master, Lord, and King, only as an instrument for the ordering of that; requires of Master, Lord, and King, the entire sharing and understanding of the hardship of that—and his fellowship with it as the only foundation of his authority over it.

'But we *have* been in it, some of us—and know it, and have, by our patience. . . .'

'Won your escape from it.' I am rude—but I know what you would say. Does then the Physician—the Artist—the Soldier—the good Priest—labour only for escape from his profession? Is not this manufacturing toil, as compared with all these, a despised one, and a miserable—by the confession of all your efforts, and the proclamation of all your pride; and will you yet go on, if it may be, to fill England, from sea to sea, with this unhappy race, out of which you have risen?

'But we cannot all be physicians, artists, or soldiers. How are we to live?'

Assuredly not in multitudinous misery. Do you think that the Maker of the world intended all but one in a thousand of His creatures to live in these dark streets; and the one, triumphant over the rest, to go forth alone into the green fields?

This was what I was thinking, and more than ever thinking, all the while my good host was driving me to Shenstone's home, The Leasowes, into the vale of Severn; and telling me how happily far away St. George's ground was, from all that is our present England's life, and—pretended—glory. As we drove down the hill a little farther, towards Bewdley (Worcester-shire for 'Beaulieu', I find—Fors undertakes for pretty names to us, it seems—Abbey-dale, Beau-lieu, and if I remember, or

---

unhappy poor to the honoured rich will be found a quite temperately expressed proportion.

translate, rightly, the House by the Fountain—our three Saxon, Norman, and Celtic beginnings of abode) my host asked me if I would like to see 'nailing'. 'Yes, truly.' So he took me into a little cottage where were two women at work—one about seventeen or eighteen, the other perhaps four or five and thirty; this last intelligent of feature as well could be; and both, gentle and kind—each with hammer in right hand, pincers in left (heavier hammer poised over her anvil, and let fall at need by the touch of her foot on a treadle like that of a common grindstone). Between them, a small forge, fed to constant brightness by the draught through the cottage, above whose roof its chimney rose: in front of it, on a little ledge, the glowing lengths of cut iron rod, to be dealt with at speed. Within easy reach of this, looking up at us in quietly silent question—stood, each in my sight an ominous *Fors*, the two *Clavigerae*.

At a word they laboured, with ancient Vulcanian skill. Foot and hand in perfect time: no dance of Muses on Parnassian mead in truer measure; no sea fairies upon yellow sands more featly footed. Four strokes with the hammer in the hand: one ponderous and momentary blow ordered of the balanced mass by the touch of the foot; and the forged nail fell aside, finished, on its proper heap; level-headed, wedge-pointed, a thousand lives soon to depend daily on its driven grip of the iron way.

So wrought they—the English Matron and Maid; so was it their darg to labour from morning to evening—seven to seven —by the furnace side—the winds of summer fanning the blast of it. The wages of the Matron Fors, I found, were eight shillings a week; her husband, otherwise and variously employed, could make sixteen. Three shillings a week for rent and taxes, left, as I count, for the guerdon of their united labour, if constant, and its product providently saved, fifty-five pounds a year, on which they had to feed and clothe themselves and their six children; eight souls in their little Worcestershire ark.

Nevertheless, I hear of all my friends pitying the distress I propose to reduce myself to, in living, all alone, upon three hundred and sixty, and doing nothing for it but contemplate the beauties of Nature; while these two poor women, with other such, pay what portion of their three shillings a week goes to provide me with my annual dividend.

Yet it was not chiefly their labour in which I pitied them, but rather in that their forge-dress did not well set off their English beauty; nay, that the beauty itself was marred by the labour; so that to most persons, who could not have looked through such veil and shadow, they were as their Master, and had no form nor comeliness. And all the while, as I watched them, I was thinking of two other Englishwomen, of about the same relative ages, with whom, in planning last *Fors*, I had been standing a little while before Edward Burne-Jones's picture of *Venus's Mirror*, and mourning in my heart for its dullness, that it, with all its Forget-me-nots, would not forget the images it bore, and take the fairer and nobler reflection of their instant life. Were these then, here—their sisters; who had only, for Venus's mirror, a heap of ashes; compassed about with no Forget-me-nots, but with the Forgetfulness of all the world?

CHAPTER I

THE SPRINGS OF WANDEL

I AM, AND MY FATHER WAS BEFORE ME, A VIOLENT TORY OF
the old school; (Walter Scott's school, that is to say, and
Homer's,) I name these two out of the numberless great Tory
writers, because they were my own two masters. I had Walter
Scott's novels and the *Iliad* (Pope's translation,) for constant
reading when I was a child, on week-days: on Sunday their
effect was tempered by *Robinson Crusoe* and the *Pilgrim's Progress*; my mother having it deeply in her heart, to make an
evangelical clergyman of me. Fortunately, I had an aunt more
evangelical than my mother; and my aunt gave me cold mutton
for Sunday's dinner, which—as I much preferred it hot—
greatly diminished the influence of the *Pilgrim's Progress*, and the
end of the matter was, that I got all the noble imaginative
teaching of Defoe and Bunyan, and yet—am not an evangelical
clergyman.

I had, however, still better teaching than theirs, and that
compulsorily, and every day of the week.

Walter Scott and Pope's Homer were reading of my own
election, and my mother forced me, by steady daily toil, to
learn long chapters of the Bible by heart; as well as to read it
every syllable through, aloud, hard names and all, from Genesis
to the Apocalypse, about once a year: and to that discipline
—patient, accurate, and resolute—I owe, not only a knowledge
of the book, which I find occasionally serviceable, but much of
my general power of taking pains, and the best part of my taste
in literature. From Walter Scott's novels I might easily, as I

grew older, have fallen to other people's novels; and Pope might, perhaps, have led me to take Johnson's English, of Gibbon's, as types of language; but, once knowing the 32nd of Deuteronomy, the 119th Psalm, the 15th of 1st Corinthians, the Sermon on the Mount, and most of the Apocalypse, every syllable by heart, and having always a way of thinking with myself what words meant, it was not possible for me, even in the foolishest times of youth, to write entirely superficial or formal English; and the affectation of trying to write like Hooker and George Herbert was the most innocent I could have fallen into.

From my own chosen masters, then, Scott and Homer, I learned the Toryism which my best after-thought has only served to confirm.

That is to say, a most sincere love of kings, and dislike of everybody who attempted to disobey them. Only, both by Homer and Scott, I was taught strange ideas about kings, which I find for the present much obsolete; for, I perceived that both the author of the *Iliad* and the author of *Waverley* made their kings, or king-loving persons, do harder work than anybody else. Tydides or Idomeneus always killed twenty Trojans to other people's one, and Redgauntlet speared more salmon than any of the Solway fishermen, and—which was particularly a subject of admiration to me—I observed that they not only did more, but in proportion to their doings, *got* less than other people—nay, that the best of them were even ready to govern for nothing! and let their followers divide any quantity of spoil or profit. Of late it has seemed to me that the idea of a king has become exactly the contrary of this, and that it has been supposed the duty of superior persons generally to govern less, and get more, than anybody else. So that it was, perhaps, quite as well that in those early days my contemplation of existent kingship was a very distant one.

The aunt who gave me cold mutton on Sundays was my

father's sister: she lived at Bridge-end, in the town of Perth, and had a garden full of gooseberry-bushes, sloping down to the Tay, with a door opening to the water, which ran past it, clear-brown over the pebbles three or four feet deep; swift-eddying—an infinite thing for a child to look down into.

My father began business as a wine-merchant, with no capital, and a considerable amount of debts bequeathed him by my grandfather. He accepted the bequest, and paid them all before he began to lay by anything for himself—for which his best friends called him a fool, and I, without expressing any opinion as to his wisdom, which I knew in such matters to be at least equal to mine, have written on the granite slab over his grave that he was 'an entirely honest merchant'. As days went on he was able to take a house in Hunter Street, Brunswick Square, No. 54 (the windows of it, fortunately for me, commanded a view of a marvellous iron post, out of which the water-carts were filled through beautiful little trap-doors, by pipes like boa-constrictors; and I was never weary of contemplating that mystery, and the delicious dripping consequent); and as years went on, and I came to be four or five years old, he could command a post-chaise and pair for two months in the summer, by help of which, with my mother and me, he went the round of his country customers (who liked to see the principal of the house his own traveller); so that, at a jog-trot pace, and through the panoramic opening of the four windows of a post-chaise, made more panoramic still to me because my seat was a little bracket in front (for we used to hire the chaise regularly for the two months out of Long Acre, and so could have it bracketed and pocketed as we liked), I saw all the high-roads, and most of the cross ones, of England and Wales, and great part of lowland Scotland, as far as Perth, where every other year we spent the whole summer; and I used to read the *Abbot at Kinross*, and the *Monastery in Glen Farg*, which I confused with *Glendearg*, and thought that the White Lady had as certainly lived by the streamlet in that glen of the Ochils, as the Queen of Scots in the island of Loch Leven.

To my further great benefit, as I grew older, I thus saw nearly all the noblemen's houses in England; in reverent and healthy delight of uncovetous admiration—perceiving, as soon as I could perceive any political truth at all, that it was probably much happier to live in a small house, and have Warwick Castle to be astonished at, than to live in Warwick Castle and have nothing to be astonished at; but that, at all events, it would not make Brunswick Square in the least more pleasantly habitable, to pull Warwick Castle down. And at this day, though I have kind invitations enough to visit America, I could not, even for a couple of months, live in a country so miserable as to possess no castles.

Nevertheless, having formed my notion of kinghood chiefly from the Fitzjames of *The Lady of the Lake*, and of *noblesse* from the Douglas there, and the Douglas in *Marmion*, a painful wonder soon arose in my child-mind, why the castles should now be always empty. Tantallon was there; but no Archibald of Angus; Stirling, but no Knight of Snowdoun. The galleries and gardens of England were beautiful to see—but his Lordship and her Ladyship were always in town, said the housekeepers and gardeners. Deep yearning took hold of me for a kind of 'Restoration', which I began slowly to feel that Charles the Second had not altogether effected, though I always wore a gilded oak-apple very piously in my button-hole on the 29th of May. It seemed to me that Charles the Second's Restoration had been, as compared with the Restoration I wanted, much as that gilded oak-apple to a real apple. And as I grew wiser, the desire for sweet pippins instead of bitter ones, and Living Kings instead of dead ones, appeared to me rational as well as romantic; and gradually it has become the main purpose of my life to grow pippins, and its chief hope, to see Kings.

I have never been able to trace these prejudices to any

royalty of descent; of my father's ancestors I know nothing, nor of my mother's more than that my maternal grandmother was the landlady of the Old King's Head in Market Street, Croydon; and I wish she were alive again, and I could paint her Simone Memmi's King's Head, for a sign.

My maternal grandfather was, as I have said, a sailor, who used to embark, like Robinson Crusoe, at Yarmouth, and come back at rare intervals, making himself very delightful at home. I have an idea he had something to do with the herring business, but am not clear on that point; my mother never being much communicative concerning it. He spoiled her, and her (younger) sister, with all his heart, when he was at home; unless there appeared any tendency to equivocation, or imaginative statements, on the part of the children, which were always unforgiveable. My mother being once perceived by him to have distinctly told him a lie, he sent the servant out forthwith to buy an entire bundle of new broom twigs to whip her with. 'They did not hurt me so much as one twig would have done,' said my mother, 'but I *thought* a good deal of it.'

My grandfather was killed at two-and-thirty, by trying to ride, instead of walk, into Croydon; he got his legs crushed by his horse against a wall; and died of the hurt's mortifying. My mother was then seven or eight years old, and, with her sister, was sent to quite a fashionable (for Croydon) day-school, Mrs. Rice's where my mother was taught evangelical principles and became the pattern girl and best needlewoman in the school; and where my aunt absolutely refused evangelical principles, and became the plague and pet of it.

My mother, being a girl of great power, with not a little pride, grew more and more exemplary in her entirely conscientious career, much laughed at, though much beloved, by her sister; who had more wit, less pride, and no conscience. At last my mother, formed into a consummate housewife, was sent for to Scotland to take care of my paternal grandfather's house; who was gradually ruining himself; and who at last, effectually ruined, and killed, himself. My father came up to London; was a clerk in a merchant's house for nine years without a holiday; then began business on his own account; paid his father's debts, and married his exemplary Croydon cousin.

Meantime my aunt had remained in Croydon, and married a baker. By the time I was four years old, and beginning to recollect things—my father rapidly taking higher commercial position in London—there was traceable—though to me, as a child, wholly incomprehensible—just the least possible shade of shyness on the part of Hunter Street, Brunswick Square, towards Market Street, Croydon. But whenever my father was ill—and hard work and sorrow had already set their mark on him—we all went down to Croydon to be petted by my homely aunt; and walk on Duppas Hill, and on the heather of Addington.

My aunt lived in the little house still standing—or which was so four months ago—the fashionablest in Market Street, having actually two windows over the shop, in the second story; but I never troubled myself about that superior part of the mansion, unless my father happened to be making drawings in indian ink, when I would sit reverently by and watch; my chosen domains being, at all other times, the shop, the bake-house, and the stones round the spring of crystal water at the back door (long since let down into the modern sewer); and my chief companion, my aunt's dog, Towzer, whom she had taken pity on when he was a snappish, starved vagrant; and made a brave and affectionate dog of: which was the kind of thing she did for every living creature that came her way, all her life long.

Contented, by help of these occasional glimpses of the rivers of Paradise, I lived until I was more than four years old in Hunter Street, Brunswick Square, the greater part of the year; for a few weeks in the summer breathing country air by taking lodgings in small cottages (real cottages, not villas, so-called) either about Hampstead, or at Dulwich, at 'Mrs. Ridley's', the last of a row in a lane which led out into the Dulwich fields on one side, and was itself full of buttercups in spring, and blackberries in autumn. But my chief remaining impressions of those days are attached to Hunter Street. My mother's general principles of first treatment were, to guard me with steady watchfulness from all avoidable pain or danger; and, for the rest, to let me amuse myself as I liked, provided I was neither fretful nor troublesome. But the law was, that I should find my own amusement. No toys of any kind were at first allowed; and the pity of my Croydon aunt for my monastic poverty in this respect was boundless. On one of my birthdays, thinking to overcome my mother's resolution by splendour of temptation, she bought the most radiant Punch and Judy she could find in all the Soho bazaar—as big as a real Punch and Judy, all dressed in scarlet and gold, and that would dance, tied to the leg of a chair. I must have been greatly impressed, for I remember well the look of the two figures, as my aunt herself exhibited their virtues. My mother was obliged to accept them; but afterwards quietly told me it was not right that I should have them; and I never saw them again.

Nor did I painfully wish, what I was never permitted for an instant to hope, or even imagine, the possession of such things as one saw in toy-shops. I had a bunch of keys to play with, as long as I was capable only of pleasure in what glittered and jingled; as I grew older, I had a cart, and a ball; and when I was five or six years old, two boxes of well-cut wooden bricks. With these modest, but, I still think, entirely sufficient possessions, and being always summarily whipped if I cried, did not do as I was bid, or tumbled on the stairs, I soon attained serene and secure methods of life and motion; and could pass my days contentedly in tracing the squares and comparing the colours of my carpet; examining the knots in the wood of the floor, or counting the bricks in the opposite houses; with rapturous intervals of excitement during the filling of the water-cart, through its leathern pipe, from the dripping iron post at the pavement edge; or the still more admirable proceedings of the turncock, when he turned and turned till a fountain sprang up in the middle of the street. But the carpet, and what patterns I could find in bed covers, dresses, or wall-papers to be examined, were my chief resources, and my attention to the particulars in these was soon so accurate, that when at three and a half I was taken to have my portrait painted by Mr. Northcote I had not been ten minutes alone with him before I asked him why there were holes in his carpet. The portrait in question represents a very pretty child with yellow hair, dressed in a white frock like a girl, with a broad light-blue sash and blue shoes to match; the feet of the child wholesomely large in proportion to its body; and the shoes still more wholesomely large in proportion to the feet.

These articles of my daily dress were all sent to the old painter for perfect realization: but they appear in the picture more remarkable than they were in my nursery, because I am represented as running in a field at the edge of a wood with the trunks of its trees striped across in the manner of Sir Joshua Reynolds; while two rounded hills, as blue as my shoes, appear in the distance, which were put in by the painter at my own request; for I had already been once, if not twice, taken to Scotland; and my Scottish nurse having always sung to me as we approached the Tweed or Esk—

For Scotland, my darling, lies full in thy view,
With her barefooted lassies, and mountains so blue,

the idea of distant hills was connected in my mind with approach to the extreme felicities of life, in my Scottish aunt's garden of gooseberry bushes, sloping to the Tay. But that, when old Mr. Northcote asked me (little thinking, I fancy, to get any answer so explicit) what I would like to have in the distance of my picture, I should have said 'blue hills' instead of 'gooseberry bushes', appears to me—and I think without any morbid tendency to think over-much of myself—a fact sufficiently curious, and not without promise, in a child of that age.

I think it should be related also that having, as aforesaid, been steadily whipped if I was troublesome, my formed habit of serenity was greatly pleasing to the old painter; for I sat contentedly motionless, counting the holes in his carpet, or watching him squeeze his paint out of its bladders—a beautiful operation, indeed, to my thinking; but I do not remember taking any interest in Mr. Northcote's application of the pigment to the canvas; my ideas of delightful art, in that respect, involving indispensably the possession of a large pot, filled with paint of the brightest green, and of a brush which would come out of it soppy. But my quietude was so pleasing to the old man that he begged my father and mother to let me sit to him for the face of a child which he was painting in a classical subject; where I was accordingly represented as reclining on a leopard skin, and having a thorn taken out of my foot by a wild man of the woods.

In all these particulars, I think the treatment, or accidental conditions, of my childhood, entirely right, for a child of my temperament: but the mode of my introduction to literature appears to me questionable, and I am not prepared to carry it out in St. George's schools, without much modification, I absolutely declined to learn to read by syllables; but would get an entire sentence by heart with great facility, and point with accuracy to every word in the page as I repeated it. As, however, when the words were once displaced, I had no more to say, my mother gave up, for the time, the endeavour to teach me to read, hoping only that I might consent, in process of years, to adopt the popular system of syllabic study. But I went on to amuse myself, in my own way, learnt whole words at a time,

as I did patterns; and at five years old was sending for my
'second volumes' to the circulating library.

This effort to learn the words in their collective aspect, was
assisted by my real admiration of the look of printed type,
which I began to copy for my pleasure, as other children draw
dogs and horses. The following inscription, facsimile'd from
the fly-leaf of my *Seven Champions of Christendom* (judging
from the independent views taken in it of the character of the
letter L, and the relative elevation of G), I believe to be an
extremely early art study of this class; and as by the will of
Fors, the first line of the note, written after an interval of fifty
years, underneath my copy of it, in direction to Mr. Burgess,
presented some notable points of correspondence with it, I
thought it well he should engrave them together, as they stood.

My mother had, as she afterwards told me, solemnly 'devoted me to God' before I was born; in imitation of Hannah.

Very good women are remarkably apt to make away with
their children prematurely, in this manner: the real meaning of
the pious act being, that, as the sons of Zebedee are not (or at
least they hope not), to sit on the right and left of Christ,
in His kingdom, their own sons may perhaps, they think, in
time be advanced to that respectable position in eternal life;
especially if they ask Christ very humbly for it every day; and
they always forget in the most naïve way that the position is
not His to give!

'Devoting me to God,' meant, as far as my mother knew
herself what she meant, that she would try to send me to
college, and make a clergyman of me: and I was accordingly
bred for 'the Church'. My father, who—rest be to his soul—
had the exceedingly bad habit of yielding to my mother in
large things and taking his own way in little ones, allowed me,
without saying a word, to be thus withdrawn from the sherry
trade as an unclean thing; not without some pardonable par-
ticipation in my mother's ultimate views for me. For, many and

many a year afterwards, I remember, while he was speaking
to one of our artist friends, who admired Raphael, and greatly
regretted my endeavours to interfere with that popular taste—
while my father and he were condoling with each other on my
having been impudent enough to think I could tell the public
about Turner and Raphael—instead of contenting myself, as I
ought, with explaining the way of their souls' salvation to them
—and what an amiable clergyman was lost in me—'Yes,' said
my father, with tears in his eyes—(true and tender tears as ever
father shed), 'he would have been a Bishop.'

Luckily for me, my mother, under these distinct impressions
of her own duty, and with such latent hopes of my future
eminence, took me very early to church; where, in spite of my
quiet habits, and my mother's golden vinaigrette, always indulged to me there, and there only, with its lid unclasped that
I might see the wreathed open pattern above the sponge, I
found the bottom of the pew so extremely dull a place to keep
quiet in (my best story-books being also taken away from me
in the morning), that, as I have somewhere said before, the
horror of Sunday used even to cast its prescient gloom as far
back in the week as Friday—and all the glory of Monday, with
church seven days removed again, was no equivalent for it.

Notwithstanding, I arrived at some abstract in my own mind
of the Rev. Mr. Howell's sermons; and occasionally, in imitation of him, preached a sermon at home over the red sofa
cushions; this performance being always called for by my
mother's dearest friends, as the great accomplishment of my
childhood. The sermon was, I believe, some eleven words long;
very exemplary, it seems to me, in that respect—and I still
think must have been the purest gospel, for I know it began
with, 'People be good'.

We seldom had company, even on week-days; and I was
never allowed to come down to dessert, until much later in
life—when I was able to crack nuts neatly. I was then permitted

to come down to crack other people's nuts for them—(I hope they liked the ministration)—but never to have any myself; nor anything else of dainty kind, either then or at other times. Once at Hunter Street, I recollect my mother giving me three raisins, in the forenoon, out of the store cabinet; and I remember perfectly the first time I tasted custard, in our lodgings in Norfolk Street—where we had gone while the house was being painted, or cleaned, or something. My father was dining in the front room, and did not finish his custard; and my mother brought me the bottom of it into the back room.

But for the reader's better understanding of such further progress of my poor little life as I may trespass on his patience in describing, it is now needful that I give some account of my father's mercantile position in London.

The firm of which he was head partner may be yet remembered by some of the older city houses, as carrying on their business in a small counting-house on the first floor of narrow premises, in as narrow a thoroughfare of East London—Billiter Street, the principal traverse from Leadenhall Street into Fenchurch Street.

The names of the three partners were given in full on their brass plate under the counting-house bell—Ruskin, Telford, and Domecq.

Mr. Domecq's name should have been the first, by rights, for my father and Mr. Telford were only his agents. He was the sole proprietor of the estate which was the main capital of the firm—the vineyard of Macharnudo, the most precious hillside, for growth of white wine, in the Spanish peninsula. The quality of the Macharnudo vintage essentially fixed the standards of Xeres 'sack', or 'dry'—*secco*—sherries, or sherry, from the days of Henry the Fifth to our own; the unalterable and unrivalled chalk-marl of it putting a strength into the grape which age can only enrich and darken—never impair.

Mr. Peter Domecq was, I believe, Spanish born; and partly

112

French, partly English bred; a man of strictest honour, and kindly disposition; how descended, I do not know; how he became possessor of his vineyard, I do not know; what position he held, when young, in the firm of Gordon, Murphy, and Company, I do not know; but in their house he watched their head clerk, my father, during his nine years of duty, and when the house broke up, asked him to be his own agent in England. My father saw that he could fully trust Mr. Domecq's honour, and feeling; but not so fully either his sense, or his industry; and insisted, though taking only his agent's commission, on being both nominally, and practically, the head-partner of the firm.

Mr. Domecq lived chiefly in Paris; rarely visiting his Spanish estate, but having perfect knowledge of the proper processes of its cultivation, and authority over its labourers almost like a chief's over his clan. He kept the wines at the highest possible standard; and allowed my father to manage all matters concerning their sale, as he thought best. The second partner, Mr. Henry Telford, brought into the business what capital was necessary for its London Branch. The premises in Billiter Street belonged to him; and he had a pleasant country house at Widmore, near Bromley; a quite far-away Kentish village in those days.

He was a perfect type of an English country gentleman of moderate fortune; unmarried, living with three unmarried sisters—who, in the refinement of their highly educated, unpretending, benevolent, and felicitous lives, remain in my memory more like the figures in a beautiful story than realities. Neither in story, nor in reality, have I ever again heard of, or seen, anything like Mr. Henry Telford—so gentle, so humble, so affectionate, so clear in common sense, so fond of horses— and so entirely incapable of doing, thinking, or saying, anything that had the slightest taint in it of the racecourse or the stable.

I

Yet I believe he never missed any great race; passed the greater part of his life on horseback; and hunted during the whole Leicestershire season; but never made a bet, never had a serious fall, and never hurt a horse. Between him and my father there was absolute confidence, and the utmost friendship that could exist without community of pursuit. My father was greatly proud of Mr. Telford's standing among the country gentlemen; and Mr. Telford was affectionately respectful to my father's steady industry and infallible commercial instinct. Mr. Telford's actual part in the conduct of the business was limited to attendance in the counting-house during two months at Midsummer, when my father took his holiday, and sometimes for a month at the beginning of the year, when he travelled for orders. At these times Mr. Telford rode into London daily from Widmore, signed what letters and bills needed signature, read the papers, and rode home again; any matters needing deliberation were referred to my father, or awaited his return. All the family at Widmore would have been limitlessly kind to my mother and me, if they had been permitted any opportunity; but my mother always felt, in cultivated society —and was too proud to feel with patience—the defects of her own early education; and therefore (which was the true and fatal sign of such defect) never familiarly visited anyone whom she did not feel to be, in some sort, her inferior.

Nevertheless, Mr. Telford had a singularly important influence in my education. By, I believe, his sister's advice, he gave me, as soon as it was published, the illustrated edition of Roger's *Italy*. This book was the first means I had of looking carefully at Turner's work: and I might, not without some appearance of reason, attribute to the gift the entire direction of my life's energies. But it is the great error of thoughtless biographers to attribute to the accident which introduces some new phase of character, and the circumstances of character which gave the accident importance. The essential point to be noted, and accounted for, was that I could understand Turner's work, when I saw it; not by what chance, or in what year, it was first seen. Poor Mr. Telford, nevertheless, was always held by papa and mamma primarily responsible for my Turner insanities.

In a more direct, though less intended way, his help to me was important. For, before my father thought it right to hire a carriage for the above-mentioned Midsummer holiday, Mr. Telford always lent us his own travelling chariot.

Now the old English chariot is the most luxurious of travelling carriages, for two persons, or even for two persons and so much of third personage as I possessed at three years old. The one in question was hung high, so that we could see well over stone dykes and average hedges out of it; such elevation being attained by the old-fashioned folding steps, with a lovely padded cushion fitting into the recess of the door—steps which it was one of my chief travelling delights to see the hostlers fold up and down; though my delight was painfully alloyed by envious ambition to be allowed to do it myself: but I never was—lest I should pinch my fingers.

The 'dickey'—(to think that I should never till this moment have asked myself the derivation of that word, and now be unable to get at it!)—being typically, that commanding seat in her Majesty's mail, occupied by the Guard; and classical, even in modern literature, as the scene of Mr. Bob Sawyer's arrangements with Sam—was thrown far back in Mr. Telford's chariot, so as to give perfectly comfortable room for the legs (if one chose to travel outside on fine days), and to afford beneath it spacious area to the boot, a storehouse of rearward miscellaneous luggage. Over which—with all the rest of forward and superficial luggage—my nurse Anne presided, both as guard and packer; unrivalled, she, in the flatness and precision of her inlaying of dresses, as in turning of pancakes; the fine precision, observe, meaning also the easy wit and invention of her art;

for, no more in packing a trunk than commanding a campaign, is precision possible without foresight.

Among the people whom one must miss out of one's life, dead, or worse than dead, by the time one is past fifty, I can only say for my own part, that the one I practically and truly miss most next to father and mother (and putting losses of imaginary good out of the question), is this Anne, my father's nurse, and mine. She was one of our 'many',[1] (our many being always but few), and from her girlhood to her old age, the entire ability of her life was given to serving us. She had a natural gift and speciality for doing disagreeable things; above all, the service of a sick room; so that she was never quite in her glory unless some of us were ill. She had also some parallel speciality for *saying* disagreeable things; and might be relied upon to give the extremely darkest view of any subject, before proceeding to ameliorative action upon it. And she had a very creditable and republican aversion to doing immediately, or in set terms, as she was bid; so that when my mother and she got old together, and my mother became very imperative and particular about having her teacup set on one side of her little round table, Anne would observantly and punctiliously put it always on the other; which caused my mother to state to me, every morning after breakfast, gravely, that if ever a woman in this world was possessed by the Devil, Anne was that woman. But in spite of these momentary and petulant aspirations to liberality and independence of character, poor Anne remained very servile in soul all her days; and was altogether occupied, from the age of fifteen to seventy-two, in doing other people's wills instead of her own, and seeking other people's good instead of her own: nor did I ever hear on any occasion of her doing harm to a human being, except by saving two hundred and some odd pounds for her relations; in consequence of which

[1] Formerly 'Meinie', 'attendant company'.

some of them, after her funeral, did not speak to the rest for several months.

The dickey then aforesaid, being indispensable for our guard Anne, was made wide enough for two, that my father might go outside also when the scenery and day were fine. The entire equipage was not a light one of its kind; but, the luggage being carefully limited, went gaily behind good horses on the then perfectly smooth mail roads; and posting, in those days, being universal, so that at the leading inns in every country town, the cry 'Horses out!' down the yard, as one drove up, was answered often instantly, always within five minutes, by the merry trot through the archway of the booted and bright-jacketed rider, with his caparisoned pair—there was no driver's seat in front: and the four large, admirably fitting and sliding windows, admitting no drop of rain when they were up, and never sticking as they were let down, formed one large moving oriel, out of which one saw the country round, to the full half of the horizon. My own prospect was more extended still, for my seat was the little box containing my clothes, strongly made, with a cushion on one end of it; set upright in front (and well forward), between my father and mother. I was thus not the least in their way, and my horizon of sight the widest possible, When no object of particular interest presented itself, I trotted, keeping time with the postboy on my trunk cushion for a saddle, and whipped my father's legs for horses; at first theoretically only, with dexterous motion of wrist; but ultimately in a quite practical and efficient manner, my father having presented me with a silver-mounted postillion's whip.

The Midsummer holiday, for better enjoyment of which Mr. Telford provided us with these luxuries, began usually on the fifteenth of May, or thereabouts—my father's birthday was the tenth; on that day I was always allowed to gather the gooseberries for his first gooseberry pie of the year, from the tree between the buttresses on the north wall of the Herne Hill garden; so that we could not leave before that *festa*. The holiday itself consisted in a tour for orders through half the English counties; and a visit (if the counties lay northwards) to my aunt in Scotland.

The mode of journeying was as fixed as that of our home life. We went from forty to fifty miles a day, starting always early enough in the morning to arrive comfortably to four o'clock dinner. Generally, therefore, getting off at six o'clock, a stage or two were done before breakfast, with the dew on the grass, and first scent from the hawthorns; if in the course of the midday drive there were any gentleman's house to be seen—or, better still, a lord's—or, best of all, a duke's—my father baited the horses, and took my mother and me reverently through the state rooms; always speaking a little under our breath to the housekeeper, major domo, or other authority in charge; and gleaning worshipfully what fragmentary illustrations of the history and domestic ways of the family might fall from their lips.

In analysing above, the effect on my mind of all this, I have perhaps a little antedated the supposed resultant impression that it was probably happier to live in a small house than a large one. But assuredly, while I never to this day pass a latticed-windowed cottage without wishing to be its cottager, I never yet saw the castle which I envied to its lord; and although in the course of these many worshipful pilgrimages I gathered curiously extensive knowledge, both of art and natural scenery, afterwards infinitely useful, it is evident to me in retrospect that my own character and affections were little altered by them; and that the personal feeling and native instinct of me had been fastened, irrevocably, long before, to things modest, humble, and pure in peace, under the low red roofs of Croydon, and by the cress-set rivulets in which the sand danced and minnows darted above the Springs of Wandel.

CHAPTER II

HERNE HILL ALMOND BLOSSOMS

WHEN I WAS ABOUT FOUR YEARS OLD MY FATHER FOUND himself able to buy the lease of a house on Herne Hill, a rustic eminence four miles south of the 'Standard in Cornhill'; of which the leafy seclusion remains, in all essential points of character, unchanged to this day: certain Gothic splendours, lately indulged in by our wealthier neighbours, being the only serious innovations; and these are so graciously concealed by the fine trees of their grounds, that the passing viator remains unappalled by them; and I can still walk up and down the piece of road between the Fox tavern and the Herne Hill station, imagining myself four years old.

Our house was the northernmost of a group which stand accurately on the top or dome of the hill, where the ground is for a small space level, as the snows are (I understand), on the dome of Mont Blanc; presently falling, however, in what may be, in the London clay formation, considered a precipitous slope, to our valley of Chamouni (or of Dulwich) on the east; and with a softer descent into Cold Harbour-lane on the west: on the south, no less beautifully declining to the dale of the Effra (doubtless shortened from Effrena, signifying the 'Un-bridled' river; recently, I regret to say, bricked over for the convenience of Mr. Biffin, chemist, and others); while on the north, prolonged indeed with slight depression some half mile or so, and receiving, in the parish of Lambeth, the chivalric title of 'Champion Hill', it plunges down at last to efface itself in the plains of Peckham, and the rural barbarism of Goose Green.

The group, of which our house was the quarter, consisted of two precisely similar partner-couples of houses, gardens and all to match; still the two highest blocks of buildings seen from Norwood on the crest of the ridge; so that the house itself, three-storied, with garrets above, commanded, in those comparatively smokeless days, a very notable view from its garret windows, of the Norwood hills on one side, and the winter sunrise over them; and of the valley of the Thames on the other, with Windsor telescopically clear in the distance, and Harrow, conspicuous always in fine weather to open vision against the summer sunset. It had front and back garden in sufficient proportion to its size; the front, richly set with old evergreens, and well-grown lilac and laburnum; the back, seventy yards long by twenty wide, renowned over all the hill for its pears and apples, which had been chosen with extreme care by our predecessor (shame on me to forget the name of the man to whom I owe so much!)—and possessing also a strong old mulberry tree, a tall white-heart cherry tree, a black Kentish one, and an almost unbroken hedge, all round, of alternate gooseberry and currant bush; decked, in due season (for the ground was wholly beneficent), with magical splendour of abundant fruit: fresh green, soft amber, and rough-bristled crimson bending the spinous branches; clustered pearl and pendent ruby joyfully discoverable under the large leaves that looked like vine.

The differences of primal importance which I observed between the nature of this garden, and that of Eden, as I had imagined it, were that, in this one, *all* the fruit was forbidden; and there were no companionable beasts: in other respects the little domain answered every purpose of Paradise to me; and the climate, in that cycle of our years, allowed me to pass most of my life in it. My mother never gave me more to learn than she knew I could easily get learnt, if I set myself honestly to work, by twelve o'clock. She never allowed anything to disturb me when my task was set; if it was not said rightly by twelve o'clock, I was kept in till I knew it, and in general, even when Latin grammar came to supplement the Psalms, I was my own master for at least an hour before half-past-one dinner, and for the rest of the afternoon.

My mother, herself finding her chief personal pleasure in her flowers, was often planting or pruning beside me, at least if I chose to stay beside *her*. I never thought of doing anything behind her back which I would not have done before her face; and her presence was therefore no restraint to me; but, also, no particular pleasure, for, from having always been left so much alone, I had generally my own little affairs to see after; and, on the whole, by the time I was seven years old, was already getting too independent, mentally, even of my father and mother; and, having nobody else to be dependent upon, began to lead a very small, perky, contented, conceited, Cock-Robinson-Crusoe sort of life, in the central point which it appeared to me (as it must naturally appear to geometrical animals), that I occupied in the universe.

This was partly the fault of my father's modesty; and partly of his pride. He had so much more confidence in my mother's judgment as to such matters than in his own, that he never ventured even to help, much less to cross her, in the conduct of my education; on the other hand, in the fixed purpose of making an ecclesiastical gentleman of me, with the superfinest of manners, and access to the highest circles of fleshly and spiritual society, the visits to Croydon, where I entirely loved my aunt, and young baker-cousins, became rarer and more rare: the society of our neighbours on the hill could not be had without breaking up our regular and sweetly selfish manner of living; and on the whole, I had nothing animate to care for, in a childish way, but myself, some nests of ants, which the gardener would never leave undisturbed for me, and a sociable bird or two; though I never had the sense or perseverance to make one really tame. But that was partly because, if ever I managed to bring one to be the least trustful of me, the cats got it.

Under these circumstances, what powers of imagination I possessed, either fastened themselves on inanimate things—the sky, the leaves, and pebbles, observable within the walls of Eden—or caught at any opportunity of flight into regions of romance, compatible with the objective realities of existence in the nineteenth century, within a mile and a quarter of Camberwell Green.

Herein, my father, happily, though with no definite intention other than of pleasing me, when he found he could do so without infringing any of my mother's rules, became my guide. I was particularly fond of watching him shave; and was always allowed to come into his room in the morning (under the one in which I am now writing), to be the motionless witness of that operation. Over his dressing-table hung one of his own watercolour drawings, made under the teaching of the elder Nasmyth; I believe, at the High School of Edinburgh. It was done in the early manner of tinting, which, just about the time when my father was at the High School, Dr. Munro was teaching Turner; namely, in grey under-tints of Prussian blue and British ink, washed with warm colour afterwards on the lights. It represented Conway Castle, with its Frith, and, in the foreground, a cottage, a fisherman, and a boat at the water's edge.

When my father had finished shaving, he always told me a story about this picture. The custom began without any initial purpose of his, in consequence of my troublesome curiosity whether the fisherman lived in the cottage, and where he was going to in the boat. It being settled, for peace'sake, that he *did* live in the cottage, and was going in the boat to fish near the castle, the plot of the drama afterwards gradually thickened; and became, I believe, involved with that of the tragedy of Douglas, and of the Castle Spectre, in both of which pieces my father had performed in private theatricals, before my mother, and a select Edinburgh audience, when he was a boy of sixteen, and she, at grave twenty, a model house-keeper, and very scornful and religiously suspicious of theat-ricals. But she was never weary of telling me, in later years, how beautiful my father looked in his Highland dress, with the high black feathers.

In the afternoons, when my father returned (always punc-tually) from his business, he dined, at half-past four, in the front parlour, my mother sitting beside him to hear the events of the day, and give counsel and encouragement with respect to the same; chiefly the last, for my father was apt to be vexed if orders for sherry fell the least short of their due standard, even for a day or two. I was never present at this time, how-ever, and only avouch what I relate by hearsay and probable conjecture; for between four and six it would have been a grave misdemeanour in me if I so much as approached the parlour door. After that, in summer time, we were all in the garden as long as the day lasted; tea under the white-heart cherry tree; or in winter and rough weather, at six o'clock in the drawing-room—I having my cup of milk, and slice of bread-and-butter, in a little recess, with a table in front of it, wholly sacred to me; and in which I remained in the evenings as an Idol in a niche, while my mother knitted, and my father read to her—and to me, so far as I chose to listen.

The series of the Waverley novels, then drawing towards its close, was still the chief source of delight in all households caring for literature; and I can no more recollect the time when I did not know them than when I did not know the Bible; but I have still a vivid remembrance of my father's intense expression of sorrow mixed with scorn, as he threw down *Count Robert of Paris*, after reading three or four pages; and knew that the life of Scott was ended: the scorn being a very complex and bitter feeling in him—partly, indeed, of the book itself, but chiefly of the wretches who were tormenting and selling the wrecked intellect, and not a little, deep down, of the subtle dishonesty which had essentially caused the ruin. My father never could forgive Scott his concealment of the Ballantyne partnership.

Such being the salutary pleasures of Herne Hill, I have next with deeper gratitude to chronicle what I owe to my mother for the resolutely consistent lessons which so exercised me in the Scriptures as to make every word of them familiar to my ear in habitual music—yet in that familiarity reverenced, as transcending all thought, and ordaining all conduct.

This she effected, not by her own sayings or personal authority; but simply by compelling me to read the book thoroughly for myself. As soon as I was able to read with fluency, she began a course of Bible work with me, which never ceased till I went to Oxford. She read alternate verses with me, watching, at first, every intonation of my voice, and correcting the false ones, till she made me understand the verse, if within my reach, rightly, and energetically. It might be beyond me altogether; that she did not care about; but she made sure that as soon as I got hold of it at all, I should get hold of it by the right end.

In this way she began with the first verse of Genesis, and went straight through, to the last verse of the Apocalypse; hard names, numbers, Levitical law, and all; and began again at Genesis the next day. If a name was hard, the better the exercise in pronunciation—if a chapter was tiresome, the better lesson in patience—if loathsome, the better lesson in faith that there was some use in its being so outspoken. After our chapters (from two to three a day, according to their length, the first thing after breakfast, and no interruption from servants allowed—none from visitors, who either joined in the reading or had to stay upstairs—and none from any visitings or excursions, except real travelling), I had to learn a few verses by heart, or repeat, to make sure I had not lost, something of what was already known; and, with the chapters thus gradually possessed from the first word to the last, I had to learn the whole body of the fine old Scottish paraphrases, which are good, melodious, and forceful verse; and to which, together with the Bible itself, I owe the first cultivation of my ear in sound.

It is strange that of all the pieces of the Bible which my mother thus taught me, that which cost me most to learn, and which was, to my child's mind, chiefly repulsive—the 119th Psalm—has now become of all the most precious to me, in its overflowing and glorious passion of love for the Law of God, in opposition to the abuse of it by modern preachers of what they imagine to be His gospel.

But it is only by deliberate effort that I recall the long morning hours of toil, as regular as sunrise—toil on both sides equal—by which, year after year, my mother forced me to learn these paraphrases, and chapters (the eighth of 1st Kings being one—try it, good reader, in a leisure hour!) allowing not so much as a syllable to be missed or misplaced; while every sentence was required to be said over and over again till she was satisfied with the accent of it. I recollect a struggle between us of about three weeks, concerning the accent of the 'of' in the lines

> Shall any following spring revive
> The ashes of the urn?—

I insisting, partly in childish obstinacy, and partly in true instinct for rhythm (being wholly careless on the subject both of urns and their contents), on reciting it with an accented *of*. It was not, I say, till after three weeks' labour, that my mother

got the accent lightened on the 'of' and laid on the ashes, to
her mind. But had it taken three years she would have done it,
having once undertaken to do it. And, assuredly, had she not
done it—well, there's no knowing what would have happened;
but I'm very thankful she *did*.

I have just opened my oldest (in use) Bible—a small, closely,
and very neatly printed volume it is, printed in Edinburgh by
Sir D. Hunter Blair and J. Bruce, Printers to the King's Most
Excellent Majesty, in 1816. Yellow, now, with age, and
flexible, but not unclean, with much use, except that the lower
corners of the pages at 8th of 1st Kings, and 32nd Deuteronomy, are worn somewhat thin and dark, the learning of
these two chapters having cost me much pains. My mother's
list of the chapters with which, thus learned, she established
my soul in life, has just fallen out of it. I will take what indulgence the incurious reader can give me, for printing the
list thus accidentally occurrent:

Exodus,	chapters	15th and 20th.
2 Samuel,	,,	1st, from 17th verse to the end.
1 Kings,	,,	8th.
Psalms,	,,	23rd, 32nd, 90th, 91st, 103rd, 112th, 119th, 139th.
Proverbs,	,,	2nd, 3rd, 8th, 12th.
Isaiah,	,,	58th.
Matthew,	,,	5th, 6th, 7th.
Acts,	,,	26th.
1 Corinthians,	,,	13th, 15th.
James,	,,	4th.
Revelation,	,,	5th, 6th.

And truly, though I have picked up the elements of a little
further knowledge—in mathematics, meteorology, and the
like, in after-life—and owe not a little to the teaching of many

people, this material installation of my mind in that property of chapters, I count very confidently the most precious, and, on the whole, the one *essential* part of all my education.

And it is perhaps already time to mark what advantage and mischief, by the chances of life up to seven years old, had been irrevocably determined for me.

I will first count my blessings (as a not unwise friend once recommended me to do, continually; whereas I have a bad trick of always numbering the thorns in my fingers and not the bones in them).

And for best and truest beginning of all blessings, I had been taught the perfect meaning of Peace, in thought, act, and word.

I never had heard my father's or mother's voice once raised in any question with each other; nor seen an angry, or even slightly hurt or offended, glance in the eyes of either. I had never heard a servant scolded; nor even, suddenly, passionately, or in any severe manner, blamed. I had never seen a moment's trouble or disorder in any household matter; nor anything whatever either done in a hurry, or undone in due time. I had no conception of such a feeling as anxiety; my father's occasional vexation in the afternoons, when he had only got an order for twelve butts after expecting one for fifteen, as I have just stated, was never manifested to *me*; and itself related only to the question whether his name would be a step higher or lower in the year's list of sherry exporters; for he never spent more than half his income, and therefore found himself little incommoded by occasional variations in the total of it. I had never done any wrong that I knew of—beyond occasionally delaying the commitment to heart of some improving sentence that I might watch a wasp on the window pane, or a bird in the cherry tree; and I had never seen any grief.

Next to this quite priceless gift of Peace, I had received the perfect understanding of the natures of Obedience and Faith. I obeyed word, or lifted finger, of father or mother, simply as a ship her helm; not only without idea of resistance, but receiving the direction as a part of my own life and force, a helpful law, as necessary to me in every moral action as the law of gravity in leaping. And my practice in Faith was soon complete: nothing was ever promised me that was not given; nothing ever threatened me that was not inflicted, and nothing ever told me that was not true.

Peace, obedience, faith; these three for chief good; next to these, the habit of fixed attention with both eyes and mind— on which I will not further enlarge at this moment, this being the main practical faculty of my life, causing Mazzini to say of me, in conversation authentically reported, a year or two before his death, that I had 'the most analytic mind in Europe'. An opinion in which, so far as I am acquainted with Europe, I am myself entirely disposed to concur.

Lastly, an extreme perfection in palate and all other bodily senses, given by the utter prohibition of cake, wine, comfits, or, except in carefullest restriction, fruit; and by fine preparation of what food was given me. Such I esteem the main blessings of my childhood; next, let me count the equally dominant calamities.

First, that I had nothing to love.

My parents were—in a sort—visible powers of Nature to me, no more loved than the sun and the moon: only I should have been annoyed and puzzled if either of them had gone out; (how much, now, when both are darkened!)—still less did I love God; not that I had any quarrel with Him, or fear of Him; but simply found what people told me was His service, disagreeable; and what people told me was His book, not entertaining. I had no companions to quarrel with, neither, nobody to assist, and nobody to thank. Not a servant was ever allowed to do anything for me, but what it was their duty to do; and why should I have been grateful to the cook for cooking, or the gardener for gardening—when the one dared not give me a baked potato without asking leave, and the other would not let my ants' nest alone, because they made the walks untidy? The evil consequence of all this was not, however, what might perhaps have been expected, that I grew up selfish or unaffectionate; but that, when affection did come, it came with violence utterly rampant and unmanageable, at least by me, who never before had anything to manage.

For (second of chief calamities) I had nothing to endure. Danger or pain of any kind I knew not; my strength was never exercised, my patience never tried, and my courage never fortified. Not that I was ever afraid of anything—either ghosts, thunder, or beasts; and one of the nearest approaches to insubordination which I was ever tempted into as a child, was in passionate effort to get leave to play with the lion's cubs in Wombell's menagerie.

Thirdly, I was taught no precision nor etiquette of manners; it was enough if, in the little society we saw, I remained unobtrusive, and replied to a question without shyness: but the shyness came later, and increased as I grew conscious of the rudeness arising from the want of social discipline, and found it impossible to acquire, in advanced life, dexterity in any bodily exercise, skill in any pleasing accomplishment, or ease and tact in ordinary behaviour.

Lastly, and chief of evils. My judgment of right and wrong, and powers of independent action, were left entirely undeveloped; because the bridle and blinkers were never taken off me. Children should have their times of being off duty, like soldiers; and when once the obedience, if required, is certain, the little creature should be very early put for periods of practice in complete command of itself; set on the bare-backed horse of its own will, and left to break it by its own strength. But the ceaseless authority exercised over my youth left me, when cast out at last into the world, unable for some time to do more than drift with its vortices.

K

My present verdict, therefore, on the general tenor of my education at that time, must be, that it was at once too formal and too luxurious; leaving my character, at the most important moment for its construction, cramped indeed, but not disciplined; and only by protection innocent, instead of by practice virtuous. My mother saw this herself, and but too clearly, in later years; and whenever I did anything wrong, stupid, or hardhearted—(and I have done many things that were all three) —always said, 'It is because you were too much indulged.'

Thus far, with some omissions, I have merely reprinted the account of these times given in *Fors*: and I fear the sequel may be more trivial, because much is concentrated in the foregoing broad statement, which I have now to continue by slower steps—and yet less amusing, because I tried always in *Fors* to say things, if I could, a little piquantly; and the rest of the things related in this book will be told as plainly as I can. But whether I succeeded in writing piquantly in *Fors* or not, I certainly wrote often obscurely; and the description given above of Herne Hill seems to me to need at once some reduction to plainer terms.

The actual height of the long ridge of Herne Hill, above Thames—at least above the nearly Thames-level of its base at Camberwell Green, is, I conceive, not more than 150 feet: but it gives the whole of this fall on both sides of it in about a quarter of a mile; forming, east and west, a succession of quite beautiful pleasure-ground and gardens, instantly dry after rain, and in which, for children, running down is pleasant play, and rolling a roller up, vigorous work. The view from the ridge on both sides, was, before railroads came, entirely lovely: westward at evening, almost sublime, over softly wreathing distances of domestic wood: Thames herself not visible, nor any fields except immediately beneath; but the tops of twenty square miles of politely inhabited groves. On the other side, east and south, the Norwood hills, partly rough with furze, partly wooded with birch and oak, partly in pure green bramble copse, and rather steep pastures, rose with the promise of all the rustic loveliness of Surrey and Kent in them, and with so much of space and height in their sweep, as gave them some fellowship with hills of true hill-districts. Fellowship now inconceivable, for the Crystal Palace, without ever itself attaining any true aspect of size, and possessing no more sublimity than a cucumber frame between two chimneys, yet by its stupidity of hollow bulk, dwarfs the hills at once; so that now one thinks of them no more but as three long lumps of clay, on lease for building. But then, the Nor-wood, or North Wood, so called as it was seen from Croydon, in opposition to the South wood of the Surrey downs, drew itself in sweeping crescent good five miles round Dulwich to the south, broken by lanes of ascent, Gipsy Hill, and others; and, from the top, commanding views towards Dartford, and over the plain of Croydon—in contemplation of which I one day frightened my mother out of her wits by saying 'the eyes were coming out of my head!' She thought it was an attack of coup-de-soleil.

Central in such amphitheatre, the crowning glory of Herne Hill was accordingly, that, after walking along its ridge southward from London through a mile of chestnut lilac, and apple trees, hanging over the wooden palings on each side— suddenly the trees stopped on the left, and out one came on the top of a field sloping down to the south into Dulwich valley—open field animate with cow and buttercup, and below, the beautiful meadows and high avenues of Dulwich; and beyond, all that crescent of the Norwood hills; a footpath, entered by a turnstile, going down to the left, always so warm that invalids could be sheltered there in March, when to walk elsewhere would have been death to them; and so quiet, that whenever I had anything difficult to compose or think of, I used to do it rather there than in our own garden. The great field was separated from the path and road only by light wooden open palings, four feet high, needful to keep the cows in. Since I last composed, or meditated there, various improvements have taken place; first the neighbourhood wanted a new church, and built a meagre Gothic one with a useless spire, for the fashion of the thing, at the side of the field; then they built a parsonage behind it, the two stopping out half the view in that direction. Then the Crystal Palace came, for ever spoiling the view through all its compass, and bringing every show-day, from London, a flood of pedestrians down the footpath, who left it filthy with cigar ashes for the rest of the week: then the railroads came, and expatiating roughs by every excursion train, who knocked the palings about, roared at the cows, and tore down what branches of blossom they could reach over the palings on the enclosed side. Then the residents on the enclosed side built a brick wall to defend themselves. Then the path got to be insufferably hot as well as dirty, and was gradually abandoned to the roughs, with a policeman on watch at the bottom. Finally, this year, a six foot high close paling has been put down the other side of it, and the processional excursionist has the liberty of obtaining what notion of the country air and prospect he may, between the wall and that, with one bad cigar before him, another behind him, and another in his mouth.

I do not mean this book to be in any avoidable way disagreeable or querulous; but expressive generally of my native disposition—which, though I say it, is extremely amiable, when I'm not bothered: I will grumble elsewhere when I must, and only notice this injury alike to the resident and excursionist at Herne Hill, because questions of right-of-way are now of constant occurrence; and in most cases, the mere *path* is the smallest part of the old Right, truly understood. The Right is of the cheerful view and sweet air which the path commanded.

Also, I may note in passing, that for all their talk about Magna Charta, very few Englishmen are aware that one of the main provisions of it is that Law should not be sold; and it seems to me that the law of England might preserve Banstead and other downs free to the poor of England, without charging me, as it has just done, a hundred pounds for its temporary performance of that otherwise unremunerative duty.

I shall have to return over the ground of these early years, to fill gaps, after getting on a little first; but will yet venture here the tediousness of explaining that my saying 'in Herne Hill garden all fruit was forbidden', only meant, of course, forbidden unless under defined restriction; which made the various gatherings of each kind in its season a sort of harvest festival; and which had this further good in its apparent severity, that, although in the at last indulgent areas, the peach which my mother gathered for me when she was sure it was ripe, and the cherry pie for which I had chosen the cherries red all round, were, I suppose, of more ethereal flavour to me than they could have been to children allowed to pluck and eat at their will; still the unalloyed and long continuing pleasure given me by our fruit-tree avenue was in its blossom, not in its bearing. For the general epicurean enjoyment of existence, potatoes well browned, green pease well boiled—broad beans of the true bitter—and the pots of damson and currant for whose annual filling we were dependent more on the greengrocer than the garden, were a hundredfold more important to me than the dozen or two of nectarines of which perhaps I might get the halves of three—(the other sides mouldy)—or the bushel or two of pears which went directly to the store-shelf. So that, very early indeed in my thoughts of trees, I had got at the principle given fifty years afterwards in *Prosperina*, that the seeds and fruits of them were for the sake of the flowers, not the flowers for the fruit. The first joy of the year being in its snowdrops, the second, and cardinal one, was in the almond blossom—every other garden and woodland gladness following from that in an unbroken order of kindling flower and shadowy leaf; and for many and many a year to come—until indeed, the whole of life became autumn to me —my chief prayer for the kindness of heaven, in its flowerful seasons, was that the frost might not touch the almond blossom.

CHAPTER III

THE BANKS OF TAY

THE READER HAS, I HOPE, OBSERVED THAT IN ALL I HAVE hitherto said, emphasis has been laid only on the favourable conditions which surround the child whose history I am writing, and on the docile and impressionable quietness of its temper.

No claim has been made for it to any special power or capacity; for, indeed, none such existed, except that patience in looking, and precision in feeling, which afterwards, with due industry, formed my analytic power.

In all essential qualities of genius, except these, I was deficient; my memory only of average power. I have literally never known a child so incapable of acting a part, or telling a tale. On the other hand, I have never known one whose thirst for visible fact was at once so eager and so methodic.

I find also that in the foregoing accounts, modest as I meant them to be, higher literature is too boastfully spoken of as my first and exclusive study. My little Pope's *Iliad*, and, in any understanding of them, my Genesis and Exodus, were certainly of little account with me till after I was ten. My calf milk of books was, on the lighter side, composed of 'Dame Wiggins of Lee', 'The Peacock at Home', and the like nursery rhymes; and on the graver side, of Miss Edgeworth's *Frank*, and *Harry and Lucy*, combined with Joyce's *Scientific Dialogues*. The earliest dated efforts I can find, indicating incipient motion of brain-molecules, are six 'poems' on subjects selected from those works; between the fourth and fifth of which my mother has written: 'January 1826. This book begun about September or October 1826, finished about January 1827.' The whole of it, therefore, was written and printed in imitation of book-print, in my seventh year. The book is a little red one, ruled with blue, six inches high by four wide, containing forty-five leaves pencilled in imitation of print on both sides— the title-page, written in the form here approximately imitated on the inside of the cover.

HARRY AND LUCY
Concluded
BEING THE LAST
Part Of
EARLY LESSONS
in four volumes
vol I
with copper
plates
PRINTED and composed by a little boy and also drawn.

Of the promised four volumes, it appears that (according to my practice to this day) I accomplished but one and a quarter, the first volume consisting only of forty leaves, the rest of the book being occupied by the aforesaid six 'poems', and the forty leaves losing ten of their pages in the 'copper plates', of which the one, purporting to represent 'Harry's new road', is, I believe, my first effort at mountain drawing. The passage closing the first volume of this work is, I think, for several reasons, worth preservation. I print it, therefore, with its own divisions of line, and three variations of size in imitated type. Punctuation must be left to the reader's kind conjecture. The hyphens, it is to be noticed, were put long or short, to make the print even, not that it ever succeeds in doing so, but the variously spaced lines here imitate it pretty well.

Harry knew very well-
what it was and went
on with his drawing but
Lucy soon called him aw-
ay and bid him observe
a great black cloud from—
the north which seemed ra
ther electrical. Harry ran
for an electrical apparatus which
his father had given him and the—
cloud electrified his apparatus positively
after that another cloud came which
electrified his apparatus negatively
and then a long train of smaller ones
but before this cloud came
a great cloud of dust rose from
the ground and followed the pos
itive cloud and at length seemed
to come in contact with it and
when the other cloud came
a flash of lightning was seen
to dart through the cloud of
dust upon which the negative
cloud spread very much and
dissolved in rain which pres
ently cleared the sky
After this phenomenon was over
and also the surprise Harry began
to wonder how electricity
could get where there was
so much water but he soon—
observed a rainbow and a—
rising mist under it which
his fancy soon transform
ed into a female form. He
then remembered the witch of
the waters at the Alps who

```
                     was raised from them by—
                     takeing some water in the—
                     hand and throwing it into
                     the air pronouncing some
                     unintelligable words. And
                     though it was a tale it—
                     affected Harry now when
                     he saw in the clouds some—
                         end of Harry      thing
                         and Lucy.      like it.
```

The several reasons aforesaid, which induce me to print this piece of, too literally, 'composition', are—the first, that it is a tolerable specimen of my seven years old spelling; tolerable only, not *fair*, since it was extremely unusual with me to make a mistake at all, whereas here there are two (takeing and unintelligable), which I can only account for by supposing I was in too great a hurry to finish my volume; the second, that the adaptation of materials for my story out of Joyce's *Scientific Dialogues* and *Manfred*, is an extremely perfect type of the interwoven temper of my mind, at the beginning of days just as much as at their end—which has always made foolish scientific readers doubt my books because there was love of beauty in them, and foolish aesthetic readers doubt my books because there was love of science in them; the third, that the extremely reasonable method of final judgment, upon which I found my claim to the sensible readers' respect for these dipartite writings, cannot be better illustrated than by this proof, that, even at seven years old, no tale, however seductive, could 'affect' Harry, until he had seen—in the clouds, or elsewhere—'something like it'.

Of the six poems which follow, the first is on the Steam-engine, beginning,

> When furious up from mines the water pours,
> And clears from rusty moisture all the ores;

and the last on the Rainbow, 'in blank verse', as being of a
didactic character, with observations on the ignorant and un-
reflective dispositions of certain people.

> But those that do not know about that light,
> Reflect not on it; and in all that light,
> Not one of all the colours do they know.

It was only, I think, after my seventh year had been fulfilled
in these meditations, that my mother added the Latin lesson
to the Bible-reading, and accurately established the daily
routine which was sketched in the foregoing chapter. But it
extremely surprises me, in trying, at least for my own amusement, if not the reader's, to finish the sketch into its corners,
that I can't recollect now what used to happen first in the
morning, except breakfasting in the nursery, and if my Croydon
cousin Bridget happened to be staying with us, quarrelling
with her which should have the brownest bits of toast. That
must have been later on, though, for I could not have been
promoted to toast at the time I am thinking of. Nothing is
well clear to me of the day's course, till, after my father had
gone to the City by the coach, and my mother's household
orders been quickly given, lessons began at half-past nine,
with the Bible readings above described, and the two or three
verses to be learned by heart, with a verse of paraphrase;—
then a Latin declension or a bit of verb, and eight words of
vocabulary from Adam's *Latin Grammar* (the best that ever
was), and the rest of the day was my own. Arithmetic was
wholesomely remitted till much later; geography I taught
myself fast enough in my own way, history was never thought
of, beyond what I chose to read of Scott's *Tales of a Grandfather*. Thus, as aforesaid, by noon I was in the garden on fine
days, or left to my own amusements on wet ones; of which
I have further at once to note that nearly as soon as I could

crawl, my toy-bricks of lignum vitæ, had been constant companions: and I am graceless in forgetting by what extravagant friend (I greatly suspect my Croydon aunt), I was afterwards gifted with a two-arched bridge, admirable in fittings of voussoir and keystone, and adjustment of the level courses of masonry with bevelled edges, into which they dovetailed, in the style of Waterloo Bridge. Well made centreings, and a course of inlaid steps down to the water, made this model largely, as accurately, instructive: and I was never weary of building, *un*building—(it was too strong to be thrown down, but had always to be *taken* down)—and rebuilding it. This inconceivable passive—or rather impassive —contentment in doing, or reading, the same thing over and over again, I perceive to have been a great condition in my future power of getting thoroughly to the bottom of matters.

Some people would say that in getting these toys lay the chance that guided me to an early love of architecture; but I never saw or heard of another child so fond of its toy bricks, except Miss Edgeworth's Frank. To be sure, in this present age—age of universal brickfield though it be—people don't give their children toy bricks, but toy puff-puffs; and the little things are always taking tickets and arriving at stations, without ever fathoming—none of them will take pains enough to do *that*—the principle of a puff-puff! And what good could they get out of it if they did—unless they could learn also, that no principle of Puff-puff would ever supersede the principle of Breath?

But I not only mastered, with Harry and Lucy, the entire motive principle of puff-puff; but also, by help of my well-cut bricks, very utterly the laws of practical stability in towers and arches, by the time I was seven years old: and these studies of structure were further animated by my invariable habit of watching, with the closest attention, the proceedings of any bricklayers, stone-sawyers, or paviours—whose work my nurse would allow me to stop to contemplate in our walks; or, delight of delights, might be seen at ease from some fortunate window of inn or lodging on our journeys. In those cases the day was not long enough for my rapturous and riveted observation.

Constantly, as aforesaid, in the garden when the weather was fine, my time there was passed chiefly in the same kind of close watching of the ways of plants. I had not the smallest taste for growing them, or taking care of them, any more than for taking care of the birds, or the trees, or the sky, or the sea. My whole time passed in staring at them, or into them. In no morbid curiosity, but in admiring wonder, I pulled every flower to pieces till I knew all that could be seen of it with a child's eyes; and used to lay up little treasures of seeds, by way of pearls and beads—never with any thought of sowing them. The old gardener only came once a week, for what sweeping and weeding needed doing; I was fain to learn to sweep the walks with him, but was discouraged and shamed by his always doing the bits I had done over again. I was extremely fond of digging holes, but that form of gardening was not allowed. Necessarily, I fell always back into my merely contemplative mind, and at nine years old began a poem, called *Eudosia*—I forget wholly where I got hold of this name, or what I understood by it—'On the Universe', though I could understand not a little by it, now. A couplet or two, as the real beginning at once of *Deucalion* and *Prosperina*, may be perhaps allowed, together with the preceding, a place in this grave memoir; the rather that I am again enabled to give accurate date—September 28th, 1828—for the beginning of its 'First book', as follows:

When first the wrath of heaven o'erwhelmed the world,
And o'er the rocks, and hills, and mountains, hurl'd
The waters' gathering mass; and sea o'er shore—
Then mountains fell, and vales, unknown before,

Lay where they were. Far different was the Earth
When first the flood came down, than at its second birth.
Now for its produce!—Queen of flowers, O rose,
From whose fair coloured leaves such odour flows,
Thou must now be before thy subjects named,
Both for thy beauty and thy sweetness famed.
Thou art the flower of England, and the flow'r
Of Beauty too—of Venus' odrous bower.
And thou wilt often shed sweet odours round,
And often stooping, hide thy head on ground.
And then the lily, towering up so proud,
And raising its gay head among the various crowd,
There the black spots upon a scarlet ground,
And there the taper-pointed leaves are found.

In 220 lines, of such quality, the first book ascends from the rose to the oak. The second begins—to my surprise, and in extremely exceptional violation of my above-boasted custom —with an ecstatic apostrophe to what I had never seen!

I sing the Pine, which clothes high Switzer's head,
And high enthroned, grows on a rocky bed,
On gulphs so deep, on cliffs that are so high,
He that would dare to climb them dares to die.

This enthusiasm, however, only lasts—mostly exhausting itself in a description, verified out of *Harry and Lucy*, of the slide of Alpnach—through seventy-six lines, when the verses cease, and the book being turned upside down, begins at the other end with the information that 'Rock-crystal is accompanied by Actynolite, Axinite, and Epidote, at Bourg d'Oisans in Dauphiny'. But the garden-meditations never ceased, and it is impossible to say how much strength was gained, or how much time uselessly given, except in pleasure, to these quiet hours and foolish rhymes. Their happiness made all the duties of outer life irksome, and their unprogressive reveries might, the reader may think, if my mother had wished, have been changed into a beginning of sound botanical knowledge. But, while there were books on geology and mineralogy which I could understand, all on botany were then—and they are little mended now—harder than the Latin grammar. The mineralogy was enough for me seriously to work at, and I am inclined finally to aver that the garden-time could not have been more rightly passed, unless in weeding.

At six punctually I joined my father and mother at tea, being, in the drawing-room, restricted to the inhabitation of the sacred niche above referred to, a recess beside the fireplace, well lighted from the lateral window in the summer evenings, and by the chimney-piece lamp in winter, and out of all inconvenient heat, or hurtful draught. A good writing-table before it shut me well in, and carried my plate and cup, or books in service. After tea, my father read to my mother what pleased themselves, I picking up what I could, or reading what I liked better instead. Thus I heard all the Shakespeare comedies and historical plays again and again—all Scott, and all *Don Quixote*, a favourite book of my father's, and at which I could then laugh to ecstasy; now, it is one of the saddest, and, in some things, the most offensive of books to me.

My father was an absolutely beautiful reader of the *best* poetry and prose; of Shakespeare, Pope, Spenser, Byron, and Scott; as of Goldsmith, Addison, and Johnson. Lighter ballad poetry he had not fineness of ear to do justice to: his sense of the strength and wisdom of true meaning, and of the force of rightly ordered syllables, made his delivery of *Hamlet*, *Lear*, *Caesar*, or *Marmion*, melodiously grand and just; but he had no idea of modulating the refrain of a ballad, and had little patience with the tenor of its sentiment. He looked always, in the matter of what he read, for heroic will and consummate reason; never tolerated the morbid love of misery for its own sake, and never read, either, for his own pleasure or my instruction, such ballads as 'Burd Helen', 'The Twa Corbies', or any other rhyme or story which sought its interest in vain love or fruitless death.

But, true, pure, and ennobling sadness began very early to mingle its undertone with the constant happiness of those days; a ballad music, beautiful in sincerity, and hallowing them like cathedral chant. Concerning which, I must go back now to the days I have only heard of with the hearing of the ear, and yet of which some are to me as if mine eyes had seen them.

It must have been a little after 1780 that my paternal grandmother, Catherine Tweeddale, ran away with my paternal grandfather when she was not quite sixteen; and my aunt Jessie, my father's only sister, was born a year afterwards; a few weeks after which event, my grandmother, not yet seventeen, was surprised, by a friend who came into her room unannounced, dancing a threesome reel, with two chairs for her partners; she having found at the moment no other way of adequately expressing the pleasure she took in this mortal life, and its gifts and promises.

The latter failed somewhat afterwards; and my aunt Jessie, a very precious and perfect creature, beautiful in her dark-eyed, Highland way—utterly religious, in her quiet Puritan way— was very submissive to Fates mostly unkind, was married to a somewhat rough tanner, with a fairly good business in the good town of Perth; and, when I was old enough to be taken first to visit them, my aunt and my uncle the tanner lived in a square-built grey-stone house in the suburb of Perth known as 'Bridge-End', the house some fifty yards north of the bridge; its garden sloping steeply to the Tay, which eddied, three or four feet deep of sombre crystal, round the steps where the servants dipped their pails.

A mistaken correspondent in *Fors* once complained of my coarse habit of sneering at people of no ancestry. I have no such

habit; though not always entirely at ease in writing of my
uncles the baker and the tanner. And my readers may trust me
when I tell them that, in now remembering my dreams in the
house of the entirely honest chief baker of Market Street, Croydon, and of Peter—not Simon—the tanner, whose house was
by the riverside of Perth, I would not change the dreams, far
less the tender realities, of those early days, for anything I hear
now remembered by lords or dames, of their days of childhood
in castle halls, and by sweet lawns and lakes in park-walled
forest.

Lawn and lake enough indeed I had, in the North Inch of
Perth, and pools of pausing Tay, before Rose Terrace (where
I used to live after my uncle died, briefly apoplectic, at Bridge-
End), in the peace of the fair Scotch summer days, with my
widowed aunt, and my little cousin Jessie, then traversing a
bright space between her sixth and ninth year; dark-eyed deeply,
like her mother, and similarly pious; so that she and I used to
compete in the Sunday evening Scriptural examinations; and
be as proud as two little peacocks because Jessie's elder brothers,
and sister Mary, used to get 'put down', and either Jessie or I
was always 'Dux'. We agreed upon this that we would be
married when we were a little older; not considering it to be
preparatorily necessary to be in any degree wiser.

Strangely, the kitchen servant-of-all-work in the house at
Rose Terrace was a very old 'Mause'—before, my grandfather's
servant in Edinburgh—who might well have been the proto-
type of the Mause of *Old Mortality*, but had even a more
solemn, fearless, and patient faith, fastened in her by extreme
suffering; for she had been nearly starved to death when she
was a girl, and had literally picked the bones out of cast-out
dust-heaps to gnaw; and ever afterwards, to see the waste of an
atom of food was as shocking to her as blasphemy. 'Oh, Miss
Margaret!' she said once to my mother, who had shaken some
crumbs off a dirty plate out of the windows, 'I had rather you

had knocked me down.' She would make her dinner upon anything in the house that the other servants wouldn't eat; often upon potato skins, giving her own dinner away to any poor person she saw; and always stand during the whole church service (though at least seventy years old when I knew her, and very feeble), if she could persuade any wild Amorite out of the streets to take her seat. Her wrinkled and worn face, moveless in resolution and patience, incapable of smile, and knit sometimes perhaps too severely against Jessie and me, if we wanted more creamy milk to our porridge, or jumped off our favourite box on Sunday ('Never mind, John,' said Jessie to me, once seeing me in an unchristian state of provocation on this subject, 'when we're married, we'll jump off boxes all day long, if we like!')—may have been partly instrumental in giving me that slight bias against Evangelical religion, which I confess to be sometimes traceable in my later works; but I never can be thankful enough for having seen, in our own 'Old Mause', the Scottish Puritan spirit in its perfect faith and force; and been enabled therefore afterwards to trace its agency in the reforming policy of Scotland, with the reverence and honour it deserves.

My aunt, a pure dove-priestess, if ever there was one, of Highland Dodona, was of a far gentler temper; but still, to me, remained at a wistful distance. She had been much saddened by the loss of three of her children before her husband's death. Little Peter, especially, had been the corner-stone of her love's building; and it was thrown down swiftly: white swelling came in the knee; he suffered much, and grew weaker gradually, dutiful always, and loving, and wholly patient. She wanted him one day to take half a glass of port wine, and took him on her knee, and put it to his lips. 'Not now, mamma; in a minute,' said he; and put his head on her shoulder, and gave one long, low sigh, and died. Then there was Catherine; and— I forget the other little daughter's name, I did not see them;

my mother told me of them; eagerly always about Catherine, who had been her own favourite. My aunt had been talking earnestly one day with her husband about these two children; planning this and that for their schooling and what not: at night, for a little while she could not sleep; and as she lay thinking, she saw the door of the room open, and two spades come into it, and stand at the foot of the bed. Both the children were dead within brief time afterwards. I was about to write 'within a fortnight'—but I cannot be sure of remembering my mother's words accurately.

But when I was in Perth, there were still—Mary, her eldest daughter, who looked after us children when Mause was too busy; James and John, William and Andrew (I can't think whom the unapostolic William was named after). But the boys were then all at school or college—the scholars, William and Andrew, only came home to tease Jessie and me, and eat the biggest jargonel pears; the collegians were wholly abstract; and the two girls and I played in our quiet ways on the North Inch, and by the 'Lead', a stream 'led' from the Tay past Rose Terrace into the town for molinary purposes; and long ago, I suppose, bricked over or choked with rubbish; but then lovely, and a perpetual treasure of flowing diamond to us children. Mary, by the way, was ascending towards twelve—fair, blue-eyed, and moderately pretty, and as pious as Jessie, without being quite so zealous.

My father rarely stayed with us in Perth, but went on business travel through Scotland, and even my mother became a curiously unimportant figure at Rose Terrace. I can't understand how she so rarely walked with us children; she and my aunt seemed always to have their own secluded ways. Mary, Jessie, and I were allowed to do what we liked on the Inch: and I don't remember doing any lessons in these Perth times, except the above-described competitive divinity on Sunday.

Had there been anybody then to teach me anything about

plants or pebbles, it had been good for me; as it was, I passed my days much as the thistles and tansy did, only with perpetual watching of all the ways of running water—a singular awe developing itself in me, both of the pools of Tay, where the water changed from brown to blue-black, and of the precipices of Kinnoull; partly out of my own mind, and partly because the servants always became serious when we went up Kinnoull way, expecially if I wanted to stay and look at the little crystal spring of Bower's Well.

'But you say you were not afraid of anything?' writes a friend, anxious for the unassailable veracity of these memoirs. Well, I said, not of ghosts, thunder or beasts—meaning to specify the commonest terrors of mere childhood. Every day, as I grew wiser, taught me a reasonable fear; else I had not above described myself as the most reasonable person of my acquaintance. And by the swirls of smooth blackness, broken by no fleck of foam, where Tay gathered herself like Medusa, I never passed without awe, even in those thoughtless days; neither do I in the least mean that I could walk among tombstones in the night (neither, for that matter, in the day), as if they were only paving stones set upright. Far the contrary; but it is important to the reader's confidence in writings which have seemed inordinately impressional and emotional, that he should know I was never subject to—I should perhaps say, sorrowfully, never capable of—any manner of illusion or false imagination, nor in the least liable to have my nerves shaken by surprise. When I was about five years old, having been on amicable terms for a while with a black Newfoundland, then on probation for watch at Herne Hill; after one of our long summer journeys my first thought on getting home was to go to see Lion. My mother trusted me to go to the stable with our one serving-man, Thomas, giving him strict orders that I was not to be allowed within stretch of the dog's chain. Thomas, for better security, carried me in his arms. Lion was at his dinner, and took no notice of either of us; on which I besought leave to pat him. Foolish Thomas stooped towards him that I might, when the dog instantly flew at me, and bit a piece clean out of the corner of my lip on the left side. I was brought up the back stairs, bleeding fast, but not a whit frightened, except lest Lion should be sent away. Lion indeed had to go; but not Thomas: my mother was sure he was sorry, and I think blamed herself the most. The bitten side of the (then really pretty) mouth, was spoiled for evermore, but the wound, drawn close, healed quickly; the last use I made of my movable lips before Dr. Aveline drew them into ordered silence for a while, was to observe, 'Mamma, though I can't speak, I can play upon the fiddle.' But the house was of another opinion, and I never attained any proficiency upon that instrument worthy of my genius. Not the slightest diminution of my love of dogs, nor the slightest nervousness in managing them, was induced by the accident.

I scarcely know whether I was in any real danger or not when another day, in the same stable, quite by myself, I went head foremost into the large water-tub kept for the garden. I think I might have got awkwardly wedged if I had tried to draw my feet in after me: instead, I used the small watering-pot I had in my hand to give myself a good thrust up from the bottom, and caught the opposite edge of the tub with my left hand, getting not a little credit afterwards for my decision of method. Looking back to the few chances that have in any such manner tried my head, I believe it has never failed me when I wanted it, and that I am much more likely to be confused by sudden admiration than by sudden danger.

The dark pools of Tay, which have led me into this boasting, were under the high bank at the head of the North Inch— the path above them being seldom traversed by us children unless at harvest time, when we used to go gleaning in the fields beyond; Jessie and I afterwards grinding our corn in the kitchen pepper-mill, and kneading and toasting for ourselves cakes of pepper bread, of quite unpurchaseable quality.

In the general course of this my careful narration, I rebut, with as much indignation as may be permitted without ill manners, the charge of partiality to anything merely because it was seen when I was young. I hesitate, however, in recording as a constant truth for the world, the impression left on me when I went gleaning with Jessie, that Scottish sheaves are more golden than are bound in other lands, and that no harvests elsewhere visible to human eyes are so like the 'corn of heaven' as those of Strath-Tay and Strath-Earn.

From *Praeterita*

CHAPTER IV

UNDER NEW TUTORSHIPS

WHEN I WAS ABOUT EIGHT OR NINE I HAD A BAD FEVERISH illness at Dunkeld, during which I believe I was in some danger, and am sure I was very uncomfortable. It came on after a long walk in which I had been gathering quantities of foxgloves and pulling them to pieces to examine their seeds, and there were hints about their having poisoned me; very absurd, but which extended the gathering awe from river eddies to foxglove dells. Not long after that, my cousin Jessie fell ill, and died very slowly of water on the brain. I was very sorry, not so much in any strength of early affection, as in the feeling that the happy days at Perth were for ever ended, since there was no more Jessie.

Before her illness took its fatal form—before, indeed, I believe it had at all declared itself—my aunt dreamed one of her foresight dreams, simple and plain enough for any one's interpretation—that she was approaching the ford of a dark river, alone, when little Jessie came running up behind her, and passed her, and went through first. Then she passed through herself, and looking back from the other side, saw old Mause approaching from the distance to the bank of the stream. And so it was, that Jessie, immediately afterwards, sickened rapidly and died; and a few months, or it might be nearly a year afterwards, my aunt died of decline; and Mause, some two or three years later, having had no care after her mistress and Jessie were gone, but when she might go to them.

I was at Plymouth with my father and mother when my

Scottish aunt died, and had been very happy with my nurse on the hill east of the town, looking out on the bay and breakwater; and came in to find my father, for the first time I had ever seen him, in deep distress of sobbing tears.

I was very sorry that my aunt was dead, but, at that time (and a good deal since, also), I lived mostly in the present, like an animal, and my principal sensation was—What a pity it was to pass such an uncomfortable evening—and we at Plymouth!

The deaths of Jessie and her mother of course ended our Scottish days. The only surviving daughter, Mary, was thenceforward adopted by my father and mother, and brought up with me. She was fourteen when she came to us, and I four years younger; so with the Perth days, closed the first decade of my life. Mary was a rather pretty, blue-eyed, clumsily-made girl, very amiable and affectionate in a quiet way, with no parts, but good sense and good principle, honestly and inoffensively pious, and equal tempered, but with no pretty girlish ways or fancies. She became a serene additional neutral tint in the household harmony; read alternate verses of the Bible with my mother and me in the mornings, and went to a day school in the forenoon. When we travelled she took somewhat of a governess position towards me, we being allowed to explore places together without my nurse; but we generally took old Anne too for better company.

It began now to be of some importance what church I went to on Sunday morning. My father, who was still much broken in health, could not go to the long Church of England service, and, my mother being evangelical, he went contentedly, or at least submissively, with her and me to Beresford Chapel, Walworth, where the Rev. D. Andrews preached, regularly, a somewhat eloquent, forcible, and ingenious sermon, not tiresome to him: the prayers were abridged from the Church Service, and we, being the grandest people in the congregation, were allowed—though, as I now remember, not without offended and reproachful glances from the more conscientious worshippers—to come in when even those short prayers were half over. Mary and I used each to write an abstract of the sermon in the afternoon, to please ourselves—Mary dutifully, and I to show how well I could do it. We never went to church in afternoon or evening. I remember yet the amazed and appalling sensation, as of a vision preliminary to the Day of Judgment, of going, a year or two later, first into a church by candlelight.

We had no family worship, but our servants were better cared for than is often the case in ostentatiously religious houses. My mother used to take them, when girls, from families known to her, sister after sister, and we never had a bad one.

On the Sunday evening my father would sometimes read us a sermon of Blair's, or it might be, a clerk or a customer would dine with us, when the conversation, in mere necessary courtesy, would take generally the direction of sherry. Mary and I got through the evening how we could, over the *Pilgrim's Progress*, Bunyan's *Holy War*, Quarle's *Emblems*, Foxe's *Book of Martyrs*, Mrs. Sherwood's *Lady of the Manor*—a very awful book to me, because of the stories in it of wicked girls who had gone to balls, dying immediately after of fever—and Mrs. Sherwood's *Henry Milner*—of which more presently—the *Youth's Magazine*, Alfred Campbell the young pilgrim, and, though rather as a profane indulgence, permitted because of the hardness of our hearts, Bingley's *Natural History*. We none of us cared for singing hymns or psalms as such, and were too honest to amuse ourselves with them as sacred music, besides that we did not find their music amusing.

My father and mother, though due cheques for charities were of course sent to Dr. Andrews, and various civilities at Christmas, in the way of turkeys or boxes of raisins, intimated their satisfaction with the style of his sermons and purity of his doctrine—had yet, with their usual shyness, never asked for his acquaintance, or even permitted the state of their souls to be inquired after in pastoral visits. Mary and I, however, were charmed merely by the distant effect of him, and used to walk with Anne up and down in Walworth, merely in the hope of seeing him pass on the other side of the way. At last, one day, when, by extreme favour of Fortune, he met us in a great hurry on our own side of it, and nearly tumbled over me, Anne, as he recovered himself, dropped him a low curtsey; whereupon he stopped, inquired who we were, and was extremely gracious to us; and we, coming home in a fever of delight, announced, not much to my mother's satisfaction, that the Doctor had said he would call some day! And so, little by little, the blissful acquaintance was made. I might be eleven or going on twelve by that time, Miss Andrews, the eldest sister of the 'Angel in the House', was an extremely beautiful girl of seventeen; she sang 'Tambourgi, Tambourgi' with great spirit and a rich voice, went at blackberry time on rambles with us at the Norwood Spa, and made me feel generally that there was something in girls that I did not understand, and that was curiously agreeable. And at last, because I was so fond of the Doctor, and he had the reputation (in Walworth) of being a good scholar, my father thought he might pleasantly initiate me in Greek, such initiation having been already too long deferred. The Doctor, it afterwards turned out, knew little more of Greek than the letters, and declensions of nouns; but he wrote the letters prettily, and had an accurate and sensitive ear for rhythm. He began me with the odes of Anacreon, and made me scan both them and my Virgil thoroughly, sometimes, by way of interlude, reciting bits of Shakespeare to me with force and propriety. The Anacreontic metre entirely pleased me, nor less the Anacreontic sentiment. I learned half the odes by heart merely to please myself, and learned with certainty, what in later study of Greek art it has proved extremely advantageous to me to know, that the

Greeks liked doves, swallows, and roses just as well as I did.

In the intervals of these unlaborious Greek lessons, I went on amusing myself—partly in writing English doggerel, partly in map drawing, or copying Cruikshank's illustrations to Grimm, which I did with great, and to most people now incredible, exactness, a sheet of them being, by good hap, well preserved, done when I was between ten and eleven. But I never saw any boy's work in my life showing so little original faculty, or grasp by memory. I could literally draw nothing, not a cat, not a boat, not a bush, 'out of my head', and there was, luckily, at present no idea on the part either of parents or preceptor, of teaching me to draw out of other people's heads.

Nevertheless, Mary, at her day school, was getting drawing lessons with other girls. Her report of the pleasantness and zeal of the master, and the frank and somewhat unusual execution of the drawings he gave her to copy, interested my father, and he was still more pleased by Mary's copying, for a proof of industry while he was away on his winter's journey—copying in pencil so as to produce the effect of a vigorous engraving, the little water-colour by Prout of a wayside cottage, which was the foundation of our future water-colour collection, being then our only possession in that kind—of other kind, two miniatures on ivory completed our gallery.

I perceive, in thinking over the good work of that patient black and white study, that Mary could have drawn if she had been well taught and kindly encouraged. But her power of patient copying did not serve her in drawing from Nature, and when, that same summer, I between ten and eleven (1829), we went to stay in Matlock in Derbyshire, all that she proved able to accomplish was an outline of Caxton's New Bath Hotel, in which our efforts in the direction of art, for that year, ended.

But in the glittering white broken spar, specked with galena, by which the walks of the hotel garden were made bright, and in the shops of the pretty village, and in many a happy walk among its cliffs, I pursued my mineralogical studies on fluor, calcite, and the ores of lead, with indescribable rapture when I was allowed to go into a cave. My father and mother showed far more kindness than I knew, in yielding to my subterranean passion; for my mother could not bear dirty places, and my father had a nervous feeling that the ladders would break, or the roof fall, before we got out again. They went with me, nevertheless, wherever I wanted to go—my father even into the terrible Speedwell mine at Castleton, where, for once, I was a little frightened myself.

From Matlock we must have gone on to Cumberland, for I find in my father's writing the legend, 'Begun 28th November, 1830, finished 11th January, 1832,' on the fly-leaf of the *Iteriad*, a poem in four books, which I indited, between those dates, on the subject of our journey among the Lakes, and of which some little notice may be taken farther on.

It must have been in the spring of 1831 that the important step was taken of giving me a drawing master. Mary showed no gift of representing any of the scenes of our travels, and I began to express some wish that I could draw myself. Whereupon, Mary's pleasant drawing master, to whom my father and mother were equitable enough to impute Mary's want of genius, was invited to give *me* also an hour in the week.

I suppose a drawing master's business can only become established by his assertion of himself to the public as the possessor of a style; and teaching in that only. Nevertheless, Mr. Runciman's memory sustains disgrace in my mind in that he gave no impulse nor even indulgence to the extraordinary gift I had for drawing delicately with the pen point. Any work of that kind was done thenceforward only to please myself. Mr. Runciman gave me nothing but his own mannered and inefficient drawings to copy, and greatly broke the force both of my mind and hand.

Yet he taught me much, and suggested more. He taught me perspective, at once accurately and simply—an invaluable bit of teaching. He compelled me into a swiftness and facility of hand which I found afterwards extremely useful, though what I have just called the 'force', the strong accuracy of my line, was lost. He cultivated in me—indeed founded—the habit of looking for the essential points in the things drawn, so as to abstract them decisively, and he explained to me the meaning and importance of composition, though he himself could not compose.

A very happy time followed, for about two years.

I was, of course, far behind Mary in touch-skill of pencil drawing, and it was good for her that this superiority was acknowledged, and due honour done her for the steady pains of her unimpulsive practice and unwearied attention. For, as she did not write poems like me, nor collect spars like me, nor exhibit any prevailing vivacity of mind in any direction, she was gradually sinking into far too subordinate a position to my high-mightiness. But I could make no pretence for some time to rival her in freehand copying, and my first attempts from Nature were not felt by my father to be the least flattering to his vanity.

These were made under a stimulus of a journey to Dover with the forethought of which my mother comforted me through an illness of 1829. I find my quite first sketch-book, an extremely inconvenient upright small octavo in mottled and flexible cover, the paper pure white, and ribbedly gritty, filled with outlines, irregularly defaced by impulsive efforts at finish, in arbitrary places and corners, of Dover and Ton-bridge Castles and the main tower of Canterbury Cathedral. These, with a really good study, supplemented by detached detail, of Battle Abbey, I have set aside for preservation; the really first sketch I ever made from nature being No. 1, of a street in Sevenoaks. I got little satisfaction and less praise by these works; but the native architectural instinct is instantly developed in these—highly notable for anyone who cares to note such nativities. Two little pencillings from Canterbury south porch and central tower, I have given to Miss Gale, of Burgate House, Canterbury; the remnants of the book itself to Mrs. Talbot, of Tyn-y-Ffynon, Barmouth, both very dear friends.

But before everything, at this time, came my pleasure in merely watching the sea. I was not allowed to row, far less to sail, nor to walk near the harbour alone; so that I learned nothing of shipping or anything else worth learning, but spent four or five hours every day in simply staring and wondering at the sea—an occupation which never failed me till I was forty. Whenever I could get to a beach it was enough for me to have the waves to look at, and hear, and pursue and fly from. I never took to natural history of shells, or shrimps, or weeds, or jellyfish. Pebbles?—yes if there were any; otherwise, merely stared all day long at the tumbling and creaming strength of the sea. Idiotically, it now appears to me, wasting all that priceless youth in mere dream and trance of admiration; it had a certain strain of Byronesque passion in it, which meant something: but it was a fearful loss of time.

The summer of 1832, must, I think, have been passed at home, for my next sketch-book contains only some efforts at tree-drawing in Dulwich, and a view over the bridge of the now bricked-up 'Effra', by which the Norwood road then crossed it at the bottom of Herne Hill: the road itself, just at the place where, from the top of the bridge, one looked up and down the streamlet, bridged now into putridly damp shade by the railway, close to Herne Hill Station. This sketch was the first in which I was ever supposed to show any talent for drawing. But on my thirteenth (?) birthday, February 8th, 1832, my father's partner, Mr. Henry Telford, gave me Rogers' *Italy*, and determined the main tenor of my life.

At that time I had never heard of Turner, except in the well remembered saying of Mr. Runciman's, that 'the world had lately been much dazzled and led away by some splendid ideas thrown out by Turner'. But I had no sooner cast eyes on the Rogers vignettes than I took them for my only masters, and set myself to imitate them as far as I possibly could by fine pen shading.

I have told this story so often that I begin to doubt its time. It is curiously tiresome that Mr. Telford did not himself write my name in the book, and my father, who writes in it, 'The gift of Henry Telford, Esq.,' still more curiously, for him puts no date: if it was a year later, no matter; there is no doubt, however, that early in the spring of 1833 Prout published his sketches in Flanders and Germany. I well remember going with my father into the shop where subscribers entered their names, and being referred to the specimen print, the turreted window over the Moselle, at Coblenz. We got the book home to Herne Hill before the time of our usual annual tour; and as my mother watched my father's pleasure and mine in looking at the wonderful places, she said, why should not we go and see some of them in reality? My father hesitated a little, then with glittering eyes said—why not? And there were two or three weeks of entirely rapturous and amazed preparation. I recollect that very evening bringing down my big geography book, still most precious to me; (I take it down now, and for the first time put my own initials under my father's name in it)—and looking with Mary at the outline of Mont Blanc, copied from Saussure, at p. 201, and reading some of the very singular information about the Alps which it illustrates. So that Switzerland must have been at once included in the plans —soon prosperously, and with result of all manner of good, by God's help fulfilled.

We went by Calais and Brussels to Cologne; up the Rhine to Strasbourg, across the Black Forest to Schaffhausen, then made a sweep through North Switzerland by Basle, Berne, Interlachen, Zürich, to Constance—following up the Rhine still to Coire, then over Splugen to Como, Milan, and Genoa; meaning, as I now remember, for Rome. But, it being June already, the heat of Genoa warned us of imprudence: we turned, and came back over the Simplon to Geneva; saw Chamouni, and so home by Lyons and Dijon.

To do all this in the then only possible way, with post-horses, and, on the lakes, with oared boats, needed careful calculation of time each day. My father liked to get to our sleeping place as early as he could, and never would stop the horses, for me to draw anything (the extra pence to postillion for waiting being also an item of weight in his mind); thus I got into the bad habit, yet not without its discipline, of making scrawls as the carriage went along, and working them up 'out of my head' in the evening. I produced in this manner, throughout the journey, some thirty sheets or so of small pen and indian ink drawings, four or five in a sheet; some not inelegant, all laborious, but for the most part one just like another, and without exception stupid and characterless to the last degree.

With these flying scrawls on the road, I made, when staying in towns, some elaborate pencil and pen outlines, of which perhaps half a dozen are worth register and preservation. My father's pride in a study of the doubly-towered Renaissance church of Dijon was great. A still more laborious *Hôtel de Ville* of Brussels remains with it at Brantwood. The drawing of that *Hôtel de Ville* by me now at Oxford is a copy of Prout's, which I made in illustration of the volume in which I wrote the beginning of a rhymed history of the tour.

For it had excited all the poor little faculties that were in me to their utmost strain, and I had certainly more passionate happiness, of a quality utterly indescribable to people who never felt the like, and more, in solid quantity, in those three months, than most people have in all their lives. The impression of the Alps first seen from Schaffhausen, of Milan and of Geneva, I will try to give some account of afterwards—my first business now is to get on.

The winter of '33, and what time I could steal to amuse myself in, out of '34, were spent in composing, writing fair, and drawing vignettes for the decoration of the aforesaid poetical account of our tour, in imitation of Rogers' *Italy*. The drawings were made on separate pieces of paper and pasted into the books; many have since been taken out, others are there for which the verses were never written, for I had spent my fervour before I got up the Rhine. I leave the unfinished folly in Joanie's care, that none but friends may see it.

Meantime, it having been perceived by my father and mother that Dr. Andrews could never prepare me for the university, nor for the duties of a bishopric, I was sent as a day scholar to the private school kept by the Rev. Thomas Dale, in Grove Lane, within walking distance of Herne Hill. Walking down with my father after breakfast, carrying my blue bag of books, I came home to half-past-one dinner, and prepared my lessons in the evening for the next day. Under these conditions I saw little of my fellow-scholars, the two sons of Mr. Dale, Tom and James; and three boarders, the sons of Colonel Matson, of Woolwich; of Alderman Key, of Denmark Hill; and a fine lively boy, Willoughby Jones, afterwards Sir W., and only lately, to my sorrow, dead.

Finding me in all respects what boys could only look upon as an innocent, they treated me as I suppose they would have treated a girl; they neither thrashed me nor chaffed me—finding, indeed, from the first that chaff had no effect on me. Generally I did not understand it, nor in the least mind it if I did, the fountain of pure conceit in my own heart sustaining me serenely against all deprecation, whether by master or companion. I was fairly intelligent of books, had a good quick and holding memory, learned whatever I was bid as fast as I could, and as well; and since all the other boys learned always as little as they could, though I was far in retard of them in real knowledge, I almost always knew the day's lesson best. I have already described in the first chapter of *Fiction Fair and Foul*, Mr. Dale's rejection of my clearly known old grammar as a 'Scotch thing'. In that one action he rejected himself from being my master; and I thenceforward learned all he told only because I had to do it.

While these steps were taken for my classical advancement, a master was found for me, still in that unlucky Walworth, to teach me mathematics. Mr. Rowbotham was an extremely industrious, deserving, and fairly well-informed person in his own branches, who, with his wife, and various impediments and inconveniences in the way of children, kept a 'young gentleman's Academy' near the Elephant and Castle, in one of the first houses which have black plots of grass in front, fenced by iron railings from the Walworth Road.

He knew Latin, German, and French grammar; was able to teach the 'use of the globes' as far as needed in a preparatory school, and was, up to far beyond the point needed for me, a really sound mathematician. For the rest, utterly unacquainted with men or their history, with Nature and its meanings; stupid and disconsolate, incapable of any manner of mirth or fancy, thinking mathematics the only proper occupation of human intellect, asthmatic to a degree causing often helpless suffering, and hopelessly poor, spending his evenings, after his school-drudgery was over, in writing manuals of arithmetic and algebra, and compiling French and German grammars, which he allowed the booksellers to cheat him out of—adding perhaps, with all his year's lamp-labour, fifteen or twenty pounds to his income; a more wretched, innocent, patient, insensible, unadmirable, uncomfortable, intolerable being never was produced in this area of England by the culture characteristic of her metropolis.

Under the tuition, twice a week in the evening, of Mr.
Rowbotham (invited always to substantial tea with us before
the lesson as a really efficient help to his hungry science, after
the walk up Herne Hill, painful to asthma), I prospered fairly
in 1834, picking up some bits of French grammar, of which
I had really felt the want—I had before got hold, somehow,
of words enough to make my way about with—and I don't
know how, but I recollect, at Paris, going to the Louvre under
charge of Salvador (I wanted to make a sketch from Rem-
brandt's *Supper at Emmaus*), and on Salvador's application to
the custode for permission, it appeared I was not old enough
to have a ticket—fifteen was then the earliest admission-age;
but seeing me look woebegone, the good-natured custode
said he thought if I went in to the 'Board', or whatever
it was, of authorities, and asked for permission myself, they
would give it me. Whereupon I instantly begged to be
introduced to the Board, and the custode taking me in under
his coat lappets, I did verily, in what broken French was
feasible to me, represent my case to several gentlemen of an
official and impressive aspect, and got my permission, and
outlined the *Supper at Emmaus* with some real success in
expression, and was extremely proud of myself. But my
narrow knowledge of the language, though thus available for
business, left me sorrowful and ashamed after the fatal dinner
at Mr. Domecq's, when the little Elise, then just nine, seeing
that her elder sisters did not choose to trouble themselves with
me, and being herself of an entirely benevolent and pitiful
temper, came across the drawing-room to me in my desolation, and leaning an elbow on my knee, set herself deliberately
to chatter to me mellifluously for an hour and a half by the
time-piece—requiring no answer, of which she saw I was
incapable, but satisfied with my grateful and respectful
attention, and admiring interest, if not exactly always in what
she said, at least in the way she said it. She gave me the entire

history of her school, and of the objectionable characters of her teachers, and of the delightful characters of her companions, and of the mischief she got into, and the surreptitious enjoyments they devised, and the joys of coming back to the Champs Elysées, and the general likeness of Paris to the Garden of Eden. And the hour and a half seemed but too short, and left me resolved, anyhow, to do my best to learn French.

So, as I said, I progressed in this study to the contentment of Mr. Rowbotham, went easily through the three first books of Euclid, and got as far as quadratics in algebra. But there I stopped, virtually, for ever. The moment I got into sums of series, or symbols expressing the relations instead of the real magnitudes of things—partly in want of faculty, partly in an already well-developed and healthy hatred of things vainly bothering and intangible—I jibbed—or stood stunned. Afterwards at Oxford they dragged me through some conic sections, of which the facts representable by drawing became afterwards of extreme value to me; and taught me as much trigonometry as made my mountain work, in plan and elevation, unaccusable. In elementary geometry I was always happy, and, for a boy, strong; and my conceit, developing now every hour more venomously as I began to perceive the weaknesses of my masters, led me to spend nearly every moment I could command for study in my own way, through the year 1835, in trying to trisect an angle. For some time afterwards I had the sense to reproach myself for the waste of thoughtful hours in that year, little knowing or dreaming how many a year to come, from that time forth, was to be worse wasted.

While the course of my education was thus daily gathering the growth of me into a stubborn standard bush, various frost-stroke was stripping away from me the poor little flowers—or herbs—of the forest, that had once grown, happily for me, at my side.

From *Praeterita*

CHAPTER V

THE SIMPLON

MORE AND MORE DEEPLY EVERY HOUR, IN RETRACING alpine paths—by my fireside—the wonder grows on me, what Heaven made the Alps for, and gave the chamois its foot, and the gentian its blue—yet gave no one the heart to love them. And in the Alps, why especially that mighty central pass was so divinely planned, yet no one to pass it but against their wills, till Napoleon came, and made a road over it.

Nor often, since, with any joy; though in truth there is no other such piece of beauty and power, full of human interest of the most strangely varied kind, in all the mountain scenery of the globe, as that traverse, with its two terminal cities, Geneva and Milan; its two lovely lakes of approach, Leman and Maggiore; its two tremendous valleys of vestibule, the Valais and Val d'Ossola; and its own, not desolate nor terrible, but wholly beautiful, upper region of rose and snow.

Of my early joy in Milan, I have already told; of Geneva, there is no telling, though I must now give what poor picture I may of the days we spent there, happy to young and old alike, again and again, in '33, '35, '42, and now, with full deliberation, in '44, knowing, and, in their repetitions twice, and thrice, and four times, magnifying, the well-remembered joys. And still I am more thankful, through every year of added life, that I was born in London, near enough to Geneva for me to reach it easily; and yet a city so contrary to everything Genevoise as best to teach me what the wonders of the little canton were.

A little canton, four miles square, and which did not wish to be six miles square! A little town, composed of a cluster of water-mills, a street of penthouses, two wooden bridges, two dozen of stone houses on a little hill, and three or four perpendicular lanes up and down the hill.

The four miles of acreage round, in grass, with modest gardens, and farm-dwelling houses; the people, pious, learned, and busy, to a man, to a woman—to a boy, to a girl, of them; progressing to and fro mostly on their feet, and only where they had business. And this bird's-nest of a place, to be the centre of religious and social thought, and of physical beauty, to all living Europe! That is to say, thinking and designing Europe—France, Germany, and Italy. They, and their pieties, and their prides, their arts and their insanities, their wraths and slaughters, springing and flowering, building and fortifying, foaming and thundering round this inconceivable point of patience: the most lovely spot, and the most notable, without any possible dispute, of the European universe; yet the nations do not covet it, do not gravitate to it—what is more wonderful, do not make a wilderness of it. They fight their battles at Chalons and Leipsic; they build their cotton mills on the Aire, and leave the Rhône running with a million of Aire power—all pure. They build their pleasure houses on Thames shingle, and Seine mud, to look across to Lambeth, and—whatever *is* on the other side of the Seine. They found their military powers in the sand of Berlin, and leave this precipice-guarded plain in peace. And yet it rules them—is the focus of thought to them, and of passion, of science, and of *contrat sociale*; of rational conduct, and of decent—and other—manners. Saussure's school and Calvin's—Rousseau's and Byron's—Turner's. . . .

And of course, I was going to say, mine; but I didn't write all that last page to end so. Yet Geneva had better have ended with educating me and the likes of me, instead of the people who have hold of it now, with their polypous knots of houses, communal with 'London, Paris, and New York'.

Beneath which, and on the esplanades of the modern casino, New York and London now live—no more the Genevese. What their home once was, I must try to tell, as I saw it.

First, it was a notable town for keeping all its poor—inside of it. In the very centre, where an English town has its biggest square, and its Exchange on the model of the Parthenon, built for the sake of the builder's commission on the cost; there, on their little pile-propped island, and by the steep lane-sides, lived the Genevoise poor; in their garrets—their laborious upper spinning or watch-wheel cutting rooms— their dark niches and angles of lane: mostly busy; the infirm and old all seen to and cared for, their porringers filled and their pallet-beds made, by household care.

But, outside the ramparts, no more poor. A sputter, perhaps, southward, along the Savoy road; but in all the champaign round, no mean rows of cubic lodgings with Doric porches; no squalid fields of mud and thistles; no deserts of abandoned brickfield and insolvent kitchen garden. On the instant, out-side Geneva gates, perfectly smooth, clean, trim-hedged or prim-walled country roads; the main broad one intent on far-away things, its signal-posts inscribed 'Route de Paris'; branching from it, right and left, a labyrinth of equally well-kept ways for fine carriage wheels, between the gentlemen's houses with their farms; each having its own fifteen to twenty to fifty acres of mostly meadow, rich-waving always (in my time for being there) with grass and flowers, like a kaleid-oscope. Stately plane trees, aspen and walnut—sometimes in avenue—casting breezy, never gloomy, shade round the dwelling-house. A dwelling-house indeed, all the year round; no travelling from it to fairer lands possible; no shutting up for seasons in town, hay-time and fruit-time, school-time and play, for generation after generation, within the cheerful white domicile with its green shutters and shingle roof— pinnacled perhaps, humorously, at the corners, glittering on

the edges with silvery tin. 'Kept up' the whole place, and all
the neighbours' places, not ostentatiously, but perfectly:
enough gardeners to mow, enough vintagers to press, enough
nurses to nurse; no foxes to hunt, no birds to shoot; but every
household felicity possible to prudence and honour, felt and
fulfilled from infancy to age.

Where the grounds came down to the waterside, they were
mostly built out into it, till the water was four or five feet deep,
lapping up, or lashing, under breeze, against the terrace wall.
Not much boating; fancy wherries, unmanageable, or too
adventurous, upon the wild blue; and Swiss boating a serious
market and trade business, unfashionable in the high rural
empyrean of Geneva. But between the Hôtel des Etrangers
(one of these country-houses open to the polite stranger, some
half-mile out of the gates, where Salvador took us in '33 and
'35) and the town, there were one or two landing-places for
the raft-like flat *feluccas*; and glimpses of the open lake and
things beyond—glimpses only, shut off quickly by garden
walls, until one came to the inlet of lake-water moat which
bent itself under the ramparts back to the city gate. This was
crossed, for people afoot who did not like going round to
that main gate, by the delicatest of filiform suspension bridges;
strong enough it looked to carry a couple of lovers over in
safety, or a nursemaid and children, but nothing heavier. One
was allowed to cross it for a centime, which seemed to me
always a most profitable transaction, the portress receiving
placidly a sort of dirty flattened sixpence (I forget its name),
and returning me a waistcoat-pocketful of the loveliest little
clean-struck centimes; and then one might stand on the
bridge any time, in perfect quiet. (The Genevese didn't like
paying the centime, and went round by the gate.) Two swans,
drifting about underneath, over a couple of fathoms of purest
green water, and the lake really opening from the moat,
exactly where the Chamouni range of *aiguilles* rose beyond it

far away. In our town walks we used always to time getting back to the little bridge at sunset, there to wait and watch.

That was the way of things on the north side; on the south, the town is still, in the main buildings of it, as then; the group of officially aristocratic houses round the cathedral and college presenting the same inaccessible sort of family dignity that they do to-day; only, since then, the Geneva Liberals—Well, I will not say what they have done; the main town stands still on its height of pebble-gravel, knit almost into rock; and still the upper terraces look across the variously mischievous Liberal works to the open southern country, rising in steady slope of garden, orchard, and vineyard—sprinkled with pretty farmhouses and bits of château, like a sea-shore with shells; rising always steeper and steeper, till the air gets rosy in the distance, then blue, and the great walnut-trees have become dots, and the farmsteads, minikin as if they were the fairy-finest of models made to be packed in a box; and then—instant—above vineyard, above farmstead, above field and wood, leaps up the Salève cliff, 2,000 feet into the air.

I don't think anybody who goes to Geneva ever sees the Salève. For the most part, no English creature ever *does* see farther than over the way; and the Salève, unless you carefully peer into it, and make out what it is, pretends to be nothing— a long, low swell like the South Downs, I fancy most people take it for, and look no more. Yet there are few rocks in the high Alps more awful than the 'Angle' of the Salève, at its foot—seven Shakespeare's Cliffs set one on top of another, and all of marble.

On the other side of the high town the houses stand closer, leaving yet space for a little sycamore-shaded walk, whence one looks down on the whole southern reach of lake, opening wide to the horizon, and edged there like the sea, but in the summer sunshine looking as if it was the one well of blue which the sunbeams drank to make the sky of. Beyond it, ghostly ranges of incredible mountains—the Dent d'Oche, and first cliffs towards Fribourg; to the west, the long wave of Jura, fading into the air above Neuchâtel.

That was the view for full noon, when the lake was brightest and bluest. Then you fell down a perpendicular lane into the lower town again, and you went to Mr. Bautte's.

Virtually there was no other jeweller in Geneva, in the great times. There were some respectable, uncompetitive shops, not dazzling, in the main street; and smaller ones, with an average supply of miniature watches, that would go well for ten years; and uncostly, but honest, trinketry. But one went to Mr. Bautte's with awe, and of necessity, as one did to one's bankers. There was scarcely any external sign of Bautte whatever—a small brass plate at the side of a narrow arched door, into an alley—into a secluded alley—leading into a monastic courtyard, out of which—or rather out of the alley, where it opened to the court, you ascended a winding stair, wide enough for two only, and came to a green door, swinging, at the top of it; and there you paused to summon courage to enter.

A not large room, with a single counter at the further side. Nothing shown on the counter. Two confidential attendants behind it, and—it might possibly be Mr. Bautte!—or his son —or his partner—or anyhow the Ruling power—at his desk beside the back window. You told what you wanted: it was necessary to know your mind, and to be sure you *did* want it; there was no showing of things for temptation at Bautte's. You wanted a bracelet, a brooch, a watch—plain or enamelled. Choice of what was wanted was quietly given. There were no big stones, no blinding galaxies of wealth. Entirely sound workmanship in the purest gold that could be worked; fine enamel for the most part, for colour, rather than jewels; and a certain Bauttesque subtlety of linked and wreathed design, which the experienced eye recognized when worn in Paris or London.

Absolutely just and moderate price; wear—to the end of your days. You came away with a sense of duty fulfilled, of treasure possessed, and of a new foundation to the respectability of your family.

You returned into the light of the open street with a blissful sense of a parcel being made up to be sent after you, and in the consequently calm expatiation of mind, went usually to watch the Rhône.

Bautte's was in the main street, out of which one caught glimpses, down the short cross ones, of the passing water, as at Sandgate, or the like fishing towns, one got peeps of the sea. With twenty steps you were beside it.

For all other rivers there is a surface, and an underneath, and a vaguely displeasing idea of the bottom. But the Rhône flows like one lambent jewel; its surface is nowhere, its ethereal self is everywhere, the iridescent rush and translucent strength of it blue to the shore, and radiant to the depth.

Fifteen feet thick, of not flowing, but flying water; not water, neither—melted glacier, rather, one should call it; the force of the ice is with it, and the wreathing of the clouds, the gladness of the sky, and the continuance of Time.

Waves of clear sea are, indeed, lovely to watch, but they are always coming or gone, never in any shape to be seen for a second. But here was one mighty wave that was always itself, and every fluted swirl of it, constant as the wreathing of a shell. No wasting away of the fallen foam, no pause for gathering of power, no helpless ebb of discouraged recoil; but alike through bright day and lulling night, the never-pausing plunge, and never-fading flash, and never-hushing whisper, and, while the sun was up, the ever-answering glow of unearthly aquamarine, ultramarine, violet-blue, gentian-blue, peacock-blue, river-of-paradise-blue, glass of a painted window melted in the sun, and the witch of the Alps flinging the spun tresses of it for ever from her snow.

The innocent way, too, in which the river used to stop to look into every little corner. Great torrents always seem angry, and great rivers too often sullen; but there is no anger, no disdain, in the Rhône. It seemed as if the mountain stream was in mere bliss at recovering itself again out of the lake sleep, and raced because it rejoiced in racing, fain yet to return and stay. There were pieces of wave that danced all day as if Perdita were looking on to learn; there were little streams that skipped like lambs and leaped like chamois; there were pools that shook the sunshine all through them, and were rippled in layers of overlaid ripples, like crystal sand; there were currents that twisted the light into golden braids, and inlaid the threads with turquoise enamel; there were strips of stream that had certainly above the lake been mill-streams, and were looking busily for mills to turn again; there were shoots of stream that had once shot fearfully into the air, and now sprang up again laughing that they had only fallen a foot or two; and in the midst of all the gay glittering and eddied lingering, the noble bearing by the midmost depth, so mighty, yet so terrorless and harmless, with its swallows skimming instead of petrels, and the dear old decrepit town as safe in the embracing sweep of it as if it were set in a brooch of sapphire.

And the day went on, as the river; but I never felt that I wasted time in watching the Rhône. One used to get giddy sometimes or discontentedly envious of the fish. Then one went back for a walk in the penthouse street, long ago gone. There was no such other street anywhere. Penthouses five stories high, not so much for the protection of the people in the street as to keep the plash of heavy rain from the house windows, so that these might be the more safely open. Beam-pillars of squared pine, with one cross-tie beam, the undecorative structural arrangement, Swiss to the very heart and pitch of it, picturesque in comfort, stately and ancient without decay, and rough, here in mid-Geneva, more than in the hill solitudes.

CHAPTER IX

THE COL DE LA FAUCILLE

ABOUT THE MOMENT IN THE FORENOON WHEN THE modern fashionable traveller, intent on Paris, Nice, and Monaco, and started by the morning mail from Charing Cross, has a little recovered himself from the qualms of his crossing, and the irritation of fighting for seats at Boulogne, and begins to look at his watch to see how near he is to the buffet of Amiens, he is apt to be baulked and worried by the train's useless stop at one inconsiderable station, lettered ABBEVILLE. As the carriage gets in motion again, he may see, if he cares to lift his eyes for an instant from his newspaper, two square towers, with a curiously attached bit of traceried arch, dominant over the poplars and osiers of the marshy level he is traversing. Such glimpse is probably all he will ever wish to get of them; and I scarcely know how far I can make even the most sympathetic reader understand their power over my own life.

The country town in which they are central—once, like Croyland, a mere monk's and peasant's refuge (so for some time called 'Refuge')—among the swamps of Somme, received about the year 650 the name of 'Abbatis Villa'—'Abbot's-ford', I had like to have written: house and village, I suppose we may rightly say—as the chief dependence of the great monastery founded by St. Riquier at his native place, on the hillside five miles east of the present town. Concerning which saint I translate from the *Dict^re des Sciences Eccles^ques*, what it may perhaps be well for the reader, in present political junctures, to remember for more weighty reasons than any arising out of such interest as he may take in my poor little nascent personality.

173

St. Riquier, in Latin *Sanctus Richarius*, born in the village of Centula, at two leagues from Abbeville, was so touched by the piety of two holy priests of Ireland, whom he had hospitably received, that he also embraced *La pénitence*. Being ordained priest, he devoted himself to preaching, and so passed into England. Then, returning into Ponthieu, he became, by God's help, powerful in work and word in leading the people to repentance. He preached at the court of Dagobert, and, a little while after that prince's death, founded the monastery which bore his name, and another, called Forest-Moutier, in the wood of Crécy, where he ended his life and penitence.

I find further in the *Ecclesiastical History of Abbeville*, published in 1646 at Paris by François Pelican, '*Rue St. Jacques, a l'enseigne du Pelican*,' that St. Riquier was himself of royal blood, that St. Angilbert, the seventh abbot, had married Charlemagne's second daughter Bertha—'*qui se rendit aussi Religieuse de l'ordre de Saint Benoist*'. Louis, the eleventh abbot, was cousin-german to Charles the Bald; the twelfth was St. Angilbert's son, Charlemagne's grandson. Raoul, the thirteenth abbot, was the brother of the Empress Judith; and Carloman, the sixteenth, was the son of Charles the Bald.

Lifting again your eyes, good reader, as the train gets to its speed, you may see gleaming opposite on the hillside the white village and its abbey—not, indeed, the walls of the home of these princes and princesses (afterwards again and again ruined), but the still beautiful abbey built on their foundations by the monks of St. Maur.

In the year when the above-quoted history of Abbeville was written (say 1600 for surety), the town, then familiarly called 'Faithful Abbeville', contained 40,000 souls, 'living in great unity among themselves, of a marvellous frankness, fearing to do wrong to their neighbour, the women modest, honest, full of faith and charity, and adorned with a goodness and beauty *toute innocente*: the noblesse numerous, hardy, and adroit in arms, the masterships (*maistrises*) of arts and trades, with excellent workers in every profession, under sixty-four Mayor-Bannerets, who are the chiefs of the trades, and elect the mayor of the city, who is an independent Home Ruler, *de grande probité, d'autorité, et sans reproche*, aided by four eschevins of the present, and four of the past year; having authority of justice, police, and war, and right to keep the weights and measures true and unchanged, and to punish those who abuse them, or sell by false weight or measure, or sell anything without the town's mark on it.' Moreover, the town contained, besides the great church of St. Wulfran, thirteen parish churches, six monasteries, eight nunneries, and five hospitals, among which churches I am especially bound to name that of St. George, begun by our own Edward in 1368, on the 10th of January; transferred and reconsecrated in 1469 by the Bishop of Bethlehem, and enlarged by the Marguilliers in 1536, 'because the congregation had so increased that numbers had to remain outside on days of solemnity'.

These reconstructions took place with so great ease and rapidity at Abbeville, owing partly to the number of its unanimous workmen, partly to the easily workable quality of the stone they used, and partly to the uncertainty of a foundation always on piles, that there is now scarce vestige left of any building prior to the fifteenth century. St. Wulfran itself, with St. Riquier, and all that remains of the parish churches (four only, now, I believe, besides St. Wulfran), are of the same flamboyant Gothic—walls and towers alike coeval with the gabled timber houses of which the busier streets chiefly consisted when first I saw them.

I must here, in advance, tell the general reader that there have been, in sum, three centres of my life's thought: Rouen, Geneva, and Pisa. All that I did at Venice was by-work, because her history had been falsely written before, and not even by any of her own people understood; and because in the world of painting, Tintoret was virtually unseen, Veronese unfelt, Carpaccio not so much as named, when I began to study them; something also was due to my love of gliding about in gondolas. But Rouen, Geneva, and Pisa have been tutresses of all I know, and were mistresses of all I did, from the first moments I entered their gates.

In this journey of 1835 I first saw Rouen and Venice—Pisa not till 1840; nor could I understand the full power of any of those great scenes till much later. But for Abbeville, which is the preface and interpretation of Rouen, I was ready on that 5th of June, and felt that here was entrance for me into immediately healthy labour and joy.

For here I saw that art (of its local kind), religion, and present human life, were yet in perfect harmony. There were no dead six days and dismal seventh in those sculptured churches; there was no beadle to lock me out of them, or pew-shutter to shut me in. I might haunt them, fancying myself a ghost; peep round their pillars like Rob Roy; kneel in them, and scandalize nobody; draw in them, and disturb none. Outside, the faithful old town gathered itself, and nestled under their buttresses like a brood beneath the mother's wings; the quiet, uninjurious aristocracy of the newer town opened into silent streets, between self-possessed hidden dignities of dwelling, each with its courtyard and richly trellised garden. The commercial square, with the main streets of traverse, consisted of uncompetitive shops, such as were needful, of the native wares: cloth and hosiery spun, woven, and knitted within the walls; cheese of neighbouring Neuchâtel; fruit of their own gardens, bread from the fields above the green *coteaux*; meat of their herds, untainted by American tin; smith's work of sufficient scythe and ploughshare, hammered on the open anvil; groceries dainty, the coffee generally roasting odoriferously in the street, before the door; for the *modistes*—well, perhaps a bonnet or two from Paris, the rest, wholesome dress for peasant and dame of Ponthieu. Above the prosperous, serenely busy and beneficent shop, the old dwelling-house of its ancestral masters; pleasantly carved, proudly roofed, keeping its place, and order, and recognized function, unfailing, unenlarging, for centuries. Round all, the breezy ramparts, with their long waving avenues through all, in various circuiting cleanness and sweetness of navigable river and active millstream, the green chalk-water of the Somme.

My most intense happinesses have of course been among mountains. But for cheerful, analloyed, unwearying pleasure, the getting in sight of Abbeville on a fine summer afternoon, jumping out in the courtyard of the Hôtel de l'Europe, and rushing down the street to see St. Wulfran again before the sun was off the towers, are things to cherish the past for—to the end.

Of Rouen, and its Cathedral, my saying remains yet to be said, if days be given me, in 'Our Fathers have told us'. The sight of them, and following journey up the Seine to Paris, then to Soissons and Rheims, determined, as aforesaid, the first centre and circle of future life-work. Beyond Rheims, at Bar-le-Duc, I was brought again within the greater radius of the Alps, and my father was kind enough to go down by Plombières to Dijon, that I might approach them by the straightest pass of Jura.

The reader must pardon my relating so much as I think he may care to hear of this journey of 1835, rather as what *used* to happen, than as limitable to that date; for it is extremely difficult for me now to separate the circumstances of any one journey from those of subsequent days, in which we stayed at the same inns, with variation only from the blue room to the green, saw the same sights, and rejoiced the more in every pleasure—that it was not new.

And this latter part of the road from Paris to Geneva, beautiful without being the least terrific or pathetic, but in the most lovable and cheerful way, became afterwards so dear and so domestic to me, that I will not attempt here to check my gossip of it.

We used always to drive out of the yard of La Cloche at

Dijon in early morning—seven, after a joyful breakfast at half-past six. The small saloon on the first floor to the front had a bedroom across the passage at the west end of it, whose windows commanded the cathedral towers over a low roof on the opposite side of the street. This was always mine, and its bed was in an alcove at the back, separated only by a lath partition from an extremely narrow passage leading from the outer gallery to Anne's room. It was a delight to Anne to which I think she looked forward all across France, to open a little hidden door from this passage, at the back of the alcove exactly above my pillow, and surprise, or wake, me in the morning.

I think I only remember once starting in rain. Usually the morning sun shone through the misty spray and far thrown diamonds of the fountain in the south-eastern suburb, and threw long poplar shadows across the road to Genlis.

Genlis, Auxonne, Dôle, Mont-sous-Vaudrey—three stages of twelve to fourteen kilometres each, two of eighteen; in all about seventy kilometres—forty-two miles, from Dijon gate to Jura foot—we went straight for the hills always, lunching on French plums and bread.

Level plain of little interest to Auxonne. I used to wonder how any mortal creature could be content to live within actual sight of Jura, and never go to see them, all their lives! At Auxonne, cross the Saone, wide and beautiful in clear shallows of green stream—little more, yet, than a noble mountain torrent; one saw in an instant it came from Jura. Another hour of patience, and from the broken yellow limestone slopes of Dôle —there, at last, they were—the long blue surges of them fading as far as eye could see to the south, more abruptly near to the north-east, where the bold outlier, almost island, of them, rises like a precipitous Wrekin, above Salins. Beyond Dôle, a new wilderness comes into the more undulating country, notable chiefly for its clay-built cottages with enormously high thatched gables of roof. Strange that I never inquired into the special reason of that form, nor looked into a single cottage to see the mode of its inhabitation!

The village, or rural town, of Poligny, clustered out of well-built old stone houses, with gardens and orchards; and gathering at the midst of it into some pretence or manner of a street, straggles along the roots of Jura at the opening of a little valley, which in Yorkshire or Derbyshire limestone would have been a gorge between nodding cliffs, with a pretty pattering stream at the bottom: but, in Jura is a far retiring theatre of rising terraces, with bits of field and garden getting foot on them at various heights; a spiry convent in its hollow, and well-built little nests of husbandry-building set in corners of meadow, and on juts of rock; no stream, to speak of, nor spring in it, nor the smallest conceivable reason for its being there, but that God made it.

'Far' retiring, I said—perhaps a mile into the hills from the outer plain, by half a mile across, permitting the main road from Paris to Geneva to serpentine and zigzag capriciously up the cliff terraces with innocent engineering, finding itself every now and then where it had no notion of getting to, and looking, in a circumflex of puzzled level, where it was to go next; retrospect of the plain of Burgundy enlarging under its backward sweeps, till at last, under a broken bit of steep final crag, it got quite up the side, and out over the edge of the ravine, where said ravine closes as unreasonably as it had opened, and the surprised traveller finds himself, magically as if he were Jack of the Beanstalk, in a new plain of an upper world. A world of level rock, breaking at the surface into yellow soil, capable of scanty, but healthy, turf, and sprinkled copse and thicket; with here and there, beyond, a blue surge of pines, and over those, if the evening or morning were clear, always one small bright silvery likeness of a cloud.

These first tracts of Jura differ in many pleasant ways from the limestone levels round Ingleborough, which are their English types. The Yorkshire moors are mostly by a hundred or two feet higher, and exposed to drift of rain under violent, nearly constant wind. They break into wide fields of loose blocks, and rugged slopes of shale; and are mixed with sand and clay from the millstone grit, which nourish rank grass, and lodge in occasional morass: the wild winds also forbidding any vestige of comfort of tree, except here and there in a sheltered nook of new plantation. But the Jura sky is as calm and clear as that of the rest of France; if the day is bright on the plain, the bounding hills are bright also; the Jura rock, balanced in the make of it between chalk and marble, weathers indeed into curious rifts and furrows, but rarely breaks loose, and has long ago clothed itself either with forest flowers, or with sweet short grass, and all blossoms that love sunshine. The pure air, even on this lower ledge of 1,000 feet above sea, cherishes their sweetest scents and liveliest colours, and the winter gives them rest under flawless serenity of snow.

A still greater and stranger difference exists in the system of streams. For all their losing themselves and hiding, and intermitting, their presence is distinctly felt on a Yorkshire moor; one sees the places they have been in yesterday, the wells where they will flow after the next shower, and a tricklet here at the bottom of a crag, or a tinkle there from the top of it, is always making one think whether this is one of the sources of Aire, or rootlets of Ribble, or beginnings of Bolton Strid, or threads of silver which are to be spun into Tees.

But no whisper, nor murmur, nor patter, nor song, of streamlet disturbs the enchanted silence of open Jura. The rain-cloud clasps her cliffs, and floats along her fields; it passes, and in an hour, the rocks are dry, and only beads of dew left in the Alchemilla leaves—but of rivulet, or brook—no vestige yesterday, or to-day, or to-morrow. Through unseen fissures and filmy crannies the waters of cliff and plain have alike vanished, only far down in the depths of the main valley glides the strong river, unconscious of change.

One is taught thus much for one's earliest lesson, in the two stages from Poligny to Champagnole, level over the absolutely crisp turf and sun-bright rock, without so much water anywhere as a cress could grow in, or a tadpole wag his tail in—and then, by a zigzag of shady road, forming the Park and Boulevard of the wistful little village, down to the single arched bridge that leaps the Ain, which pauses underneath in magnificent pools of clear pale green: the green of spring leaves; then clashes into foam, half weir, half natural cascade, and into a confused race of currents beneath hollow overhanging of crag festooned with leafage. The only marvel is, to anyone knowing Jura structure, that rivers should be visible anywhere at all, and that the rocks should be consistent enough to carry them in open air through the great valleys, without perpetual *pertes* like that of the Rhône. Below the Lac de Joux the Orbe thus loses itself indeed, reappearing 700 feet beneath in a scene of which I permit myself to quote my Papa Saussure's description.

'A semicircular rock at least 200 feet high, composed of great horizontal rocks hewn vertical, and divided by ranks of pine which grow on their projecting ledges, closes to the west the valley of Valorbe. Mountains yet more elevated and covered with forests, form a circuit round this rock, which opens only to give passage to the Orbe, whose source is at its foot. Its waters, of a perfect limpidity, flow at first with a majestic tranquillity upon a bed tapestried with beautiful green moss (*Fontinalis antipyretica*), but soon, drawn into a steep slope, the thread of the current breaks itself in foam against the rocks which occupy the middle of its bed, while the borders, less agitated, flowing always on their green ground, set off the whiteness of the midst of the river; and thus it withdraws itself from sight, in following the course of a deep valley covered with pines, whose blackness is rendered more striking by the vivid green of the beeches which are scattered among them.

'Ah, if Petrarch had seen this spring and had found there his Laura, how much would not he have preferred it to that of Vaucluse, more abundant, perhaps, and more rapid, but of which the sterile rocks have neither the greatness of ours, nor the rich parure, which embellishes them.'

I have never seen the source of the Orbe, but would commend to the reader's notice the frequent beauty of these great springs in literary *rising* at the base of cliffs, instead of falling, as one would have imagined likely, out of the clefts in the front of them. In our own English antitype of the source of Orbe, Malham Cove, the flow of water is, in like manner, wholly at the base of the rock, and seems to rise to the ledge of its outlet from a deeper interior pool.

The old Hôtel de la Poste at Champagnole stood just above the bridge of Ain, opposite the town, where the road got level again as it darted away towards Geneva. I think the year 1842 was the first in which we lengthened the day from Dijon by the two stages beyond Poligny; but afterwards, the Hôtel de la Poste became a kind of home to us; going out, we had so much delight there, and coming home, so many thoughts, that a great space of life seemed to be passed in its peace. No one was ever in the house but ourselves; if a family stopped every third day or so, it was enough to maintain the inn, which, besides, had its own farm; and those who did stop, rushed away for Geneva early in the morning. We, who were to sleep again at Morez, were in no hurry; and in returning always left Geneva on Friday, to get the Sunday at Champagnole.

But my own great joy was in the early evening, when we had arrived from Dijon, and I got out after the quickly dressed trout and cutlet for the first walk on rock and under pine.

With all my Tory prejudice (I mean, principle), I have to confess that one great joy of Swiss—above all, Jurassic Swiss—ground to me, is in its effectual, not merely theoretic, *liberty*. Among the greater hills, one can't always go just where one chooses—all around is the too far or too steep—one wants to get to this, and climb that, and can't do either; but in Jura one can go every way, and be happy everywhere. Generally, if there was time, I used to climb the islet of crag to the north of the village, on which there are a few grey walls of ruined castle, and the yet traceable paths of its 'pleasance', whence to look if the likeness of white cloud were still on the horizon. Still there, in the clear evening, and again and again, each year more marvellous to me; the *derniers rochers*, and *calotte* of Mont Blanc. Only those; that is to say just as much as may be seen over the Dome du Gouté from St. Martin's. But it looks as large from Champagnole as it does there—glowing in the last light like a harvest moon.

If there were not time to reach the castle rock, at least I could get into the woods above Ain, and gather my first Alpine flowers. Again and again, I feel the duty of gratitude to the formalities and even vulgarities of Herne Hill, for making me to feel by contrast the divine wildness of Jura forest.

Then came the morning drive into the higher glen of the Ain, where the road began first to wind beside the falling stream. One never understands how those winding roads steal with their tranquil slope from height to height; it was but an hour's walking beside the carriage—an hour passed like a minute: and one emerged on the high plain of St. Laurent, and the gentians began to gleam among the roadside grass, and the pines swept round the horizon with the dark infinitude of ocean.

All Switzerland was there in hope and sensation, and what was less than Switzerland was in some sort better, in its meek simplicity and healthy purity. The Jura cottage is not carved with the stately richness of the Bernese, nor set together with the antique strength of Uri. It is covered with thin slit fine shingles side-roofed as it were to the ground for mere dryness' sake, a little crossing of laths here and there underneath the window its only ornament. It has no daintiness of garden nor wealth of farm about it—is indeed little more than a delicately-built chalet, yet trim and domestic, mildly intelligent of things other than pastoral, watch-making and the like, though set in the midst of the meadows, the gentian at its door, the lily of the valley wild in the copses hard by.

My delight in these cottages, and in the sense of human industry and enjoyment through the whole scene, was at the root of all pleasure in its beauty; see the passage written afterwards in the *Seven Lamps* insisting on this as if it were general to human nature thus to admire through sympathy. I have noticed since, with sorrowful accuracy, how many people there are who, wherever they find themselves, think only 'of their position'. But the feeling which gave me so much happiness, both then and through life, differed also curiously, in its impersonal character, from that of many even of the best and kindest persons.

In the beginning of the Carlyle-Emerson correspondence, edited with too little comment by my dear friend Charles Norton, I find at page 18 this—to me entirely disputable, and to my thought, so far as undisputed, much blameable and pitiable, exclamation of my master's: 'Not till we can think that here and there one is thinking of us, does this waste earth become a peopled garden.' My training, as the reader has perhaps enough perceived, produced in me the precisely opposite sentiment. *My* times of happiness had always been when *nobody* was thinking of me; and the main discomfort and drawback to all proceedings and designs, the attention and interference of the public—represented by my mother and the gardener. The garden was no waste place to me, because I did not suppose myself an object of interest either to the ants or the butterflies; and the only qualification of the entire delight of my evening's walk at Champagnole or St. Laurent was the sense that my father and mother *were* thinking of me, and would be frightened if I were five minutes late for tea.

I don't mean in the least that I could have done without them. They were, to me, much more than Carlyle's wife to him; and if Carlyle had written, instead of, that he wanted Emerson to think of him in America, that he wanted his father and mother to be thinking of him at Eclefechan, it had been well. But that the rest of the world was waste to him unless he had admirers in it, is a sorry state of sentiment enough; and I am somewhat tempted, for once, to admire the exactly opposite temper of my own solitude. My entire delight was in observing without being myself noticed—if I could have been invisible, all the better. I was absolutely interested in men and their ways, as I was interested in marmots and chamois, in tomtits and trouts. If only they could stay still and let me look at them, and not get into their holes and up their heights! The living inhabitation of the world—the grazing and nesting in it—the spiritual power of the air, the rocks, the waters, to be in the midst of it, and rejoice and wonder at it, and help it if I could—happier if it needed no help of mine—this was the essential love of *Nature* in me, this the root of all that I have usefully become, and the light of all that I have rightly learned.

Whether we slept at St. Laurent or Morez, the morning of the next day was an eventful one. In ordinarily fine weather, the ascent from Morez to Les Rousses, walked most of the way, was mere enchantment; so also breakfast, and fringed-gentian gathering, at Les Rousses. Then came usually an hour of tortured watching the increase of the noon clouds; for, however early we had risen, it was impossible to reach the Col de la Faucille before two o'clock, or later if we had bad horses, and at two o'clock, if there are clouds above Jura, there will be assuredly clouds on the Alps.

It is worth notice, Saussure himself not having noticed it, that this main pass of Jura, unlike the great passes of the Alps, reaches its highest traverse-point very nearly under the highest summit of that part of the chain. The *col*, separating the source of the Bienne, which runs down to Morez and St. Claude, from that of the Valserine, which winds through the midst of Jura to the Rhône at Bellegarde, is a spur of the Dôle itself, under whose prolonged masses the road is then carried six miles farther, ascending very slightly to the Col de la Faucille, where the chain opens suddenly, and a sweep of the road, traversed in five minutes at a trot, opens the whole Lake of Geneva, and the chain of the Alps along 100 miles of horizon.

I have never seen that view perfectly but once—in this year 1835; when I drew it carefully in my then fashion, and have been content to look back to it as the confirming sequel of the first view of the Alps from Schaffhausen. Very few travellers, even in old times, saw it at all; tired of the long posting journey from Paris, by the time they got to the col they were mostly thinking only of their dinners and rest at Geneva; the guide books said nothing about it; and though, for everybody, it was an inevitable task to ascend the Righi, nobody ever thought there was anything to be seen from the Dôle.

Both mountains have had enormous influence on my whole life; the Dôle continually and calmly; the Righi at sorrowful intervals, as will be seen. But the Col de la Faucille, on that day of 1835, opened to me in distant vision the Holy Land of my future work and true home in this world. My eyes had been opened, and my heart with them, to see and to possess royally such a kingdom! Far as the eye could reach—that land and its moving or pausing waters; Arve, and his gates of Cluse, and his glacier fountains; Rhône, and the infinitude of his sapphire lake—his peace beneath the narcissus meads of Vevay—his cruelty beneath the promontories of Sierre. And all that rose against and melted into the sky, of mountain and mountain snow; and all that living plain, burning with human gladness— studded with white homes—a milky way of star-dwellings cast across its sunlight blue.

CHAPTER X

QUEM TU MELPOMENE

WHAT THE FURROW AT CHRIST CHURCH WAS TO BE LIKE, or where to lead, none of my people seem at this time to have been thinking. My mother, watching the naturalistic and methodic bent of me, was, I suppose, tranquil in the thought of my becoming another White of Selborne, or Vicar of Wakefield, victorious in Whistonian and every other controversy. My father perhaps conceived more cometic or meteoric career for me, but neither of them put the matter seriously in hand, however deeply laid up in heart: and I was allowed without remonstrance to go on measuring the blue of the sky, and watching the flight of the clouds, till I had forgotten most of the Latin I ever knew, and all the Greek, except Anacreon's ode to the rose.

Some little effort was made to pull me together in 1836 by sending me to hear Mr. Dale's lectures at King's College, where I explained to Mr. Dale, on meeting him one day in the court of entrance, that porticoes should not be carried on the top of arches; and considered myself exalted because I went in at the same door with boys who had square caps on. The lectures were on early English literature, of which, though I had never read a word of any before Pope, I thought myself already a much better judge than Mr. Dale. His quotation of 'Knut the king came sailing by' stayed with me; and I think that was about all I learnt during the summer. For, as my adverse stars would have it, that year my father's partner, Mr. Domecq, thought it might for once be expedient that he should himself pay a complimentary round of visits to his British customers, and asked if meanwhile he might leave his daughters at Herne Hill to see the lions at the Tower, and so on. How we got them all into Herne Hill corners and cupboards would be inexplicable but with a plan of the three stories! The arrangements were half Noah's ark, half Doll's house, but we got them all in: Clotilde, a graceful oval-faced blonde of fifteen; Cécile, a dark, finely-browed, beautifully-featured girl of thirteen; Elise, again fair, round-faced like an English girl, a treasure of good nature and good sense; Caroline, a delicately quaint little thing of eleven. They had all been born abroad, Clotilde at Cadiz, and of course convent-bred; but lately accustomed to be much in society during vacation at Paris. Deeper than any one dreamed, the sight of them in the Champs Elysées had sealed itself in me, for they were the first well-bred and well-dressed girls I had ever seen—or at least spoken to. I mean of course, by well-dressed, perfectly simply dressed, with Parisian cutting and fitting. They were all 'bigoted'—as Protestants would say— quietly firm, as they ought to say—Roman Catholics; spoke Spanish and French with perfect grace, and English with broken precision: were all fairly sensible, Clotilde sternly and accurately so, Elise gaily and kindly, Cécile serenely, Caroline keenly. A most curious galaxy, or southern cross, of unconceived stars, floating on a sudden into my obscure firmament of London suburb.

How my parents could allow their young novice to be cast into the fiery furnace of the outer world in this helpless manner the reader may wonder, and only the Fates know; but there was this excuse for them, that they had never seen me the least interested or anxious about girls—never caring to stay in the promenades at Cheltenham or Bath, or on the parade at Dover; on the contrary, growling and mewing if I was ever kept there, and off to the sea or the fields the moment I got leave; and they had educated me in such extremely orthodox English Toryism and Evangelicalism that they could not conceive their scientific, religious, and George the Third revering youth, wavering in his constitutional balance towards French Catholics. And I had never *said* anything about the Champs Elysées! Virtually convent-bred more closely than the maids themselves, without a single sisterly or cousinly affection for refuge or lightning rod, and having no athletic skill or pleasure to check my dreaming, I was thrown, bound hand and foot, in my unaccomplished simplicity, into the fiery furnace, or fiery cross, of these four girls—who of course reduced me to a mere heap of white ashes in four days. Four days, at the most, it took to reduce me to ashes, but the *Mercredi des cendres* lasted four years.

Anything more comic in the externals of it, anything more tragic in the essence, could not have been invented by the skilfullest designer in either kind. In my social behaviour and mind I was a curious combination of Mr. Traddles, Mr. Toots, and Mr. Winkle. I had the real fidelity and single-mindedness of Mr. Traddles, with the conversational abilities of Mr. Toots, and the heroic ambition of Mr. Winkle; all these illuminated by imagination like Mr. Copperfield's, at his first Norwood dinner.

Clotilde (Adèle Clotilde in full, but her sisters called her Clotilde, after the queen-saint, and I Adèle, because it rhymed to shell, spell, and knell) was only made more resplendent by the circlet of her sisters' beauty; while my own shyness and unpresentableness were farther stiffened, or rather sanded, by a patriotic and Protestant conceit, which was tempered neither by politeness nor sympathy; so that, while in company I sate jealously miserable like a stock of fish (in truth, I imagine, looking like nothing so much as a skate in an aquarium trying to get up the glass), on any blessed occasion of *tête-à-tête* I endeavoured to entertain my Spanish-born, Paris-bred, and Catholic-hearted mistress with my own views upon the subjects of the Spanish

Armada, the Battle of Waterloo, and the doctrine of Transubstantiation.

To these modes of recommending myself, however, I did not fail to add what display I could make of the talents I supposed myself to possess. I wrote with great pains, and straining of my invention, a story about Naples (which I had never seen), and 'the Bandit Leoni'. whom I represented as typical of what my own sanguinary and adventurous disposition would have been had I been brought up a bandit; and 'the Maiden Giuletta', in whom I portrayed all the perfections of my mistress. Our connection with Messrs. Smith & Elder enabled me to get this story printed in *Friendships' Offering;* and Adèle laughed over it in rippling ecstasies of derision, of which I bore the pain bravely, for the sake of seeing her thoroughly amused.

I dared not address any sonnets straight to herself; but when she went back to Paris, wrote her a French letter seven quarto pages long, descriptive of the desolations and solitudes of Herne Hill since her departure. This letter, either Elise or Caroline wrote to tell me she had really read, and 'laughed immensely at the French of'. Both Caroline and Elise pitied me a little, and did not like to say she had also laughed at the contents.

The old people, meanwhile, saw little harm in all this. Mr. Domecq, who was extremely good-natured, and a good judge of character, rather liked me, because he saw that I was good-natured also, and had some seedling brains, which would come up in time: in the interests of the business he was perfectly ready to give me any of his daughters I liked, who could also be got to like me, but considered that the time was not come to talk of such things. My father was entirely of the same mind, besides being pleased at my getting a story printed in *Friendship's Offering*, glad that I saw something of girls with good manners, and in hopes that if I wrote poetry about them, it might be as good as the Hours of Idleness. My mother, who looked upon the idea of my marrying a Roman Catholic as too monstrous to be possible in the decrees of Heaven, and too preposterous to be even guarded against on earth, was rather annoyed at the whole business, as she would have been if one of her chimneys had begun smoking—but had not the slightest notion her house was on fire. She saw more, however, than my father, into the depth of the feeling, but did not, in her motherly tenderness, like to grieve me by any serious check to it. She hoped, when the Domecqs went back to Paris, we might see no more of them and that Adèle's influence and memory would pass away—with next winter's snow.

Under these indulgent circumstances—bitterly ashamed of the figure I had made, but yet not a whit dashed back out of my daily swelling foam of furious conceit, supported as it was by real depth of feeling, and (note it well, good reader) by a true and glorious sense of the newly revealed miracle of human love, in its exaltation of the physical beauty of the world I had till then sought by its own light alone—I set myself in that my seventeenth year, in a state of majestic imbecility, to write a tragedy on a Venetian subject, in which the sorrows of my soul were to be enshrined in immortal verse—the fair heroine, Bianca, was to be endowed with the perfections of Desdemona, and the brightness of Juliet—and Venice and Love were to be described, as never had been thought of before. I may note in passing, that on my first sight of the Ducal Palace, the year before, I had deliberately announced to my father and mother, and—it seemed to me stupidly incredulous—Mary, that I meant to make such a drawing of the Ducal Palace as never had been made before. This I proceeded to perform by collecting some hasty memoranda on the spot, and finishing my design elaborately out of my head at Treviso. The drawing still exists—for a wonder, out of perspective, which I had now got too conceited to follow the rules of—and with the diaper pattern of the red and white marbles represented as a bold panelling in relief. No figure disturbs the solemn tranquillity of the Riva, and the gondolas—each in the shape of a Turkish crescent standing on its back on the water—float about without the aid of gondoliers.

I remember nothing more of that year, 1836, than sitting under the mulberry tree in the back garden, writing my tragedy. I forget whether we went travelling or not, or what I did in the rest of the day. It is all now blank to me, except Venice, Bianca, and looking out over Shooter's Hill, where I could see the last turn of the road to Paris.